THE COMEBACK KING
DONALD TRUMP'S UNFINISHED BUSINESS

Table of Contents

CATHERINE MCCARTHY

CATHERINE MCCARTHY

Disclaimer

Although the author has made every effort to ensure that the information in this book was correct at press time and while this publication is designed to provide accurate information in regard to the subject matter covered, the author assumes no responsibility for errors, inaccuracies, omissions, or any other inconsistencies herein and hereby disclaim any liability to any party for any loss, damage, or disruption caused by errors or omissions.

THE COMEBACK KING: DONALD TRUMP'S UNFINISHED BUSINESS

Cover Design by Atindra Nath Publisher Catherine McCarthy

First edition, 2023.

ABOUT THE AUTHOR

Catherine McCarthy is based in Sydney, Australia and has written a number of short stories and magazine articles. Whilst planning this book, she created two fun coloring books for Donald Trump fans.

"The Comeback King" is her first non-fiction piece. *The rise of Donald Trump was a fascinating enigma that demanded exploration.* Driven by a desire to comprehend the intricacies of American politics and the societal factors that allowed such an unconventional candidate to secure the highest office in the land, she embarked on a journey of extensive research and analysis.

Dedication

To my ever-patient husband for his belief and undying support and love.

THE COMEBACK KING: DONALD TRUMP'S UNFINISHED BUSINESS

CHAPTER 1

THE ENTREPRENEUR

THE COMEBACK KING: DONALD TRUMP'S UNFINISHED BUSINESS

"All of the women on 'The Apprentice' Flirted with me - consciously or unconsciously. That's to be expected."

~Trump: *How To Get Rich*, 2004

IN 1990, Donald Trump's life continued to be mired in controversy. Though he was a decade away from becoming a reality television star, his real life provided plenty of fodder for tabloids and more serious news outlets alike.

Financial crises

Trump was forced to navigate the murky waters of a global recession brought on by a collapse of the world's financial systems. The seemingly endless growth of the 1980s had come to a screeching halt. Trump, like many other entrepreneurs, faced spiraling debt as the market went through a paradigm shift.

There were many reasons for the financial collapse in the West. First, America was flooded with cheaply manufactured goods from Asia, particularly China. The U.S. was rapidly losing ground to Japan in terms of technological advancement.

And finally, the 'voodoo economics' of Ronald Reagan led the middle class to dwindle while more people were living below the poverty line.

Donald Trump was in a better position than most to protect his assets during the recession, yet even he was not immune to its deleterious effects. It is estimated that by 1990, Trump had incurred more than three and a half billion dollars worth of debt, though he himself was only responsible for $800 million of that amount. While many of his brethren crashed and burned during this period, the ever-resourceful and cunning Trump found ways to keep the lights on and the money flowing into his coffers.

One of the major changes Trump made during this period was to focus less on building his real estate empire. Instead, he made his focus on turning himself into a household name brand. Call it fame or infamy, but in the 1990s, as now, people just couldn't seem to stop talking about Trump. He took advan- tage of this media climate to launch numerous ventures branded under his name.

The move came at just the right time because Trump, like many others in this period, was suffering the effects of the global recession. The early nineties were particularly fraught with hardship for the Don.

His Castle casino and hotel lost more than ninety million in the fiscal year from 1990 to 1991. This mirrored problems with his other casinos, which hemorrhaged money to the tune of $30,000. Only through savvy business sense was he able to avoid losing the empire he had worked so hard to build in the 70s and 80s.

His interest payments totaled more than seventeen million, and he had fallen four million in his tax payments to state and federal agencies. He was even forced to surrender his airline, which had been tanking badly. Undaunted, Trump found many creative ways to stay in business.

He coaxed his father, Fred Trump, into purchasing millions in casino chips from the Castle, which were kept uncashed. Trump also took out loans from his family members. Lastly, he used the public's growing fascination with his life and brand to keep the revenue flowing and his business empire afloat.

Even thirty years before his presidency, Trump was leaning hard into his boisterous personality to generate both media attention and revenue—although he was positively sedate compared to his persona during his election campaign and presidency.

Trump also took advantage of the United State's labyrinthian and complex tax laws. Shrewdly using deductions and incentives, he saved millions of dollars.

During his 2016 presidential campaign, at a rally in Colorado, Trump said the following:

"I was able to use the tax laws in this country and my business acumen to dig out of the real-estate mess—you would call it a depression—when few others were able to do what I did."

While all of these clever plans helped Trump stave off the metaphorical wolves at his door, his greatest stroke of genius was taking his Atlantic City casino holdings public. By offering stock in these companies, he generated a monumental amount of revenue. It seemed like everyone wanted in on the Trump gravytrain.

As difficult as his financial woes were in the 1990s, Trump's personal life was perhaps worse.

Trump's Personal Life

His long-time marriage to Ivana was on the rocks. Donald Trump began to appear in public with Marla Maples, a swimsuit model, and former Miss Hawaiian Tropic. Despite the fact that he was still married to Ivana, Trump made no secret of his intimacy with Maples. The two became heavy tabloid fodder both in print and on television shows such as *A Current A!air.*

Eventually, the cracks started to show overtly in Trump's marriage to Ivana. In 1991, she filed for divorce. To further add to the chaos and media frenzy surrounding the Donald Trump brand, Ivana went on a whirlwind press tour presenting herself as the long-suffering ex-wife victimized by her husband.

She would tell a gossip column in 1991, *"The children are all wrecks; Ivanka now comes home from school crying, 'Mommy, does it mean I'm not going to be Ivanka Trump anymore?' Little Eric asks me, 'Is it true you are going away and not coming back?'"*

Undaunted by the bad press and judgmental tabloid head- lines, Trump would weather the divorce and marry Marla Maples in 1993. At first, the couple seemed happy, but after the birth of their daughter Tiffany, it looked as if the Don would soon be heading back to divorce court—yet again.

His marriage to Marla Maples crumbled under the unbear- able weight of public scrutiny. Citing irreconcilable differences, the couple filed for divorce in 1997.

Trump's divorce became nigh constant fuel for the media frenzy that followed. Wild speculation about his marriage to Ivana, and subsequent divorce, didn't seem to get the Don down. In fact, he seemed to revel in his status as a tabloid icon and cult of personality.

"The show is Trump, and it is sold-out performances every- where." *Playboy*, 1990.

Donald Trump would not stay single for long. In 1998 he met model Melania Knauss, an immigrant whose beauty no doubt reminded him of Marla Maples. The two began a rela- tionship, though they would not wed until 2005. Perhaps

Donald Trump had wanted to be absolutely sure before walking the aisle a third time with a new bride.

Trump expertly handled the media following his divorce and a subsequent shake-up in his love life. There's an old adage that says there is no such thing as bad press. Even negative stories were used to build up the Trump brand and keep him fresh in the minds of the public and investors in his casino enterprises.

Trump's savvy with crafting his public persona coincided with his branching out into new ventures. He acquired golf courses and lent his famous moniker to a number of products. Thanks to the public's voracious appetite for details about his life – and Trump's constant stoking of those appetites – he was able to remain a prominent figure in the New York City real estate scene.

This isn't to say that Trump didn't face controversy and challenges in other arenas as well. With the Trump brand on everyone's lips, it's not surprising that those in his orbit began to look for ways to cash in.

In 1991, John O'Donnell, former president of Trump Plaza Hotel and Casino in Atlantic City, published a tell-all memoir that focused a great deal on The Don's dealings. One passage in the book proved particularly troubling for Trump and caused a great deal of controversy.

John O'Donnel alleged a conversation he'd had with his boss Trump concerning an African American accountant who worked for the casino.

THE COMEBACK KING: DONALD TRUMP'S UNFINISHED BUSINESS

"Black guys counting my money! I hate it. The only kind of people I want counting my money are short guys that wear yarmulkes every day. ... I think that the guy is lazy. And it's probably not his fault, because laziness is a trait in blacks. It really is, I believe that. It's not anything they can control."

While the quote remains unsubstantiated, it mired Trump

in further controversy. His troubles were far from over with regard to allegations of racial prejudice.

In 1992 Trump Plaza Hotel and Casino was forced to pay a fine of $2,000.

The fine resulted from casino officials forcing female and people of color dealers to vacate gaming tables to accommodate a high-rolling guest's prejudices. Though Trump was not directly involved in the incident, it still reflected poorly on him in the media.

Trump was also accused of being racist toward Native Americans. He believed that Natives opening casinos on reser- vation land would provide competition and a possible death blow to his own gambling houses. Trump took out an advertise- ment alleging that members of certain Native American tribes were irredeemably corrupt and would be unable to run the casinos fairly. His appeal to Congress to block the Native casinos would ultimately fail, though the impact on his own businesses remains unclear.

Perhaps the most famous example of Trump's alleged prej- udice comes as a result of the Central Park Five. In 1989, five teenagers – four black and one Hispanic – were charged with the assault of a woman in Central Park. Trump famously took out a full-page ad in the newspapers, demanding a return of the death penalty, and condemned the young men as being guilty before their trial had even concluded.

Years later, DNA evidence would exonerate the Central Park Five, but many of Trump's detractors would point to the incident as being a low point in his race relations.

Trump also had to contend with allegations of business misconduct and fraudulent practices. He attempted to buy a controlling interest in two rival Atlantic City casinos, a scheme that is far from illegal and happens every day on the market.

However, regulations dictated that Trump inform the

THE COMEBACK KING: DONALD TRUMP'S UNFINISHED BUSINESS

Federal Trade Commission about such large stock purchases, and he failed to do so. The resulting scandal damaged the Don's reputation further. Eventually, the Federal Trade Commission took Donald Trump to court and forced him to pay three-quarters of a million dollars to settle the matter.

In spite of these challenges, however, Trump managed to maintain his hold on his business empire, tenuous as it may have seemed at the time. He used his cult of personality and tabloid celebrity status to his advantage during this period and managed to weather the 1990s, if not unscathed, then at the least in a stronger position than many of his contemporaries.

While his legacy is likely to be viewed through the lens of his presidency, his life before becoming president is also notable for the ups and downs of his business career, his success in the media, and his personal relationships.

CHAPTER 2

THE PATH TO THE WHITE

HOUSE

CATHERINE MCCARTHY

THE COMEBACK KING: DONALD TRUMP'S UNFINISHED BUSINESS

DONALD TRUMP'S journey to becoming president of the United States was a long and unconventional one, marked by controversy, divisiveness, and unexpected twists and turns.

There is a particular career path most politicians follow: Start off involved in the local branch of your political party affil- iation. Work your way up from the grunt work of fetching coffee to doing the more white-collar aspects of the political game. Then, after you've developed a good reputation among your local party affiliates, put your name up for nomination to a local office.

From there, the expected trajectory takes you from local political offices to state offices and the national level. Certainly, it's unusual for someone to gain the office of the presidency without first having served in Congress.

Donald Trump eschewed this conventional trajectory, a move in line with his idiom and personal brand. Simply put, the Don follows his own path. While sometimes it can seem chaotic, it does seem to lead to success again and again, even after tragedy and downfall.

While he didn't run for office in the 1980s, Donald Trump became heavily involved in the New York City political scene. He often railed against policies and practices that he believed harmed his business interests.

One area where Donald Trump was particularly vociferous was the concept of rent control. He argued that in some of his holdings, rent-controlled units barely paid enough to cover his operational costs.

This led to a particularly ugly fight over a fourteen-story building at 100 Central Park South. Trump bought the building to demolish it and erect a larger, more modern and profitable structure.

However, he had to contend with legacy renters, many of whom had been in the building for most of their natural lives. One man, an interior designer, had a six-bedroom luxury apart- ment for which he only paid around nine hundred dollars monthly. Even in the 80s, this was an astonishingly low rent for such a prime piece of real estate.

Lawsuits bounded back and forth between Trump and his tenants. The tenants claimed Trump stopped all repairs to the building and allowed trash and rodents to infest the structure. Trump claimed the lawsuits were frivolous and intended to draw attention away from the fact many of the tenants had ille- gally modified their apartments before he took over the building. In the end, it should be pointed out that no public agency ever found any evidence of wrongdoing on Trump's part or the part of Citadel management, to whom he outsourced the day- to-day operations of the apartment building. However, Trump did settle with the tenants in civil court, paying half a million in total to their attorneys.

Trump believed the idea of rent control was harmful not just to himself and his own interests but to New York as a whole. But soon, real estate would not be the only thing Trump focused upon.

As the decade wore on, Trump began to grow more inter- ested in international affairs. In an interview with Dr. Bernard Lown, The Don professed a desire to be made the ambassador plenipotentiary to Moscow. His goal was rather ambitious—to put an end to the Cold War.

Trump believed that the then-communist country would see him as a neutral party. While his plans never came to fruition, it's clear that his interest in Russia and peacemaking began long before he took the oath of o$ce.

But the clearest indication of overt political ambitions came in 1988. During a much-ballyhooed speech to the Portsmouth, New Hampshire Rotary Club, Trump expressed a great deal of dissatisfaction with the way the United States was conducting its business on the world stage.

Despite the fact that many people in the audience carried signs declaring *Trump for President '88*, the Don would disap- point them by announcing he would not be running as a candi- date. He praised candidates George H.W. Bush, Michael Dukakis, and Jesse Jackson before delivering a warning to the gathered crowd – most of whom weren't even part of the Portsmouth Rotary Club:

"If the right man doesn't get into o!ce, you're going to see a catastrophe in this country in the next four years like you're

never going to believe. And then you'll be begging for the right man."

At this point, Trump had not yet declared himself to be the 'right man' for the job, but he had a lot of opinions on the matter. While many were disappointed by his refusal to run for president in 1988, his rhetoric also encouraged them, which echoed a growing sentiment that America was backsliding from its former glory.

It was during this era that Trump declared himself a staunch Republican – though there were some caveats to that statement.

When world-renowned interviewer and 1980s Icon Larry King asked Trump if he was a "Bush Republican," the Don vehemently denied it:

"No. The people that I do best with drive the taxis. You know, wealthy people don't like me because I'm competing with them all the time. And I like to win. I go down the streets of New York and the people that really like me are the workers."

Trump's answer would echo his later sentiments when he ran for the highest office in 2016, during which he made a point to portray himself as an anti-elitist man of the people.

In 1999, Donald Trump began to flirt with the idea of putting himself forward as a presidential candidate. It would take a former pro wrestler and action movie star to prompt him into throwing his hat into the ring.

Jesse "The Body" Ventura had cut his teeth in the pro wrestling ring and co-starred with Arnold Schwarzenegger in some of the 1980s' biggest movies. His foray into politics was initially met with scorn and derision – just like Donald Trump's would be almost two decades later.

To everyone's surprise, except maybe Jesse Ventura's, the former bodybuilder not only won the governor's race for

Minnesota, but he also proved to be a capable and adept leader. Ventura focused on a populist message when he campaigned. He saw himself as a champion of middle America and the forgotten center, voters who did not see themselves as either left or rightwing. Ventura was part of the Reform Party, a political entity formed originally by Billionaire Ross Perot in the 1992 presi- dential election. While Perot failed to win a single state's elec- toral votes, he did put out impressive numbers for an independent candidate. The Reform Party would continue to exist, though it eventually swung from economic to more social causes.

Donald Trump met with Jesse Ventura, and the former grilled the governor for details on winning political office. Despite some initial skepticism, Ventura would be won over by the Don's earnestness and purported desire to make a change for the better in America. Ventura became Trump's most vocal proponent in the Reform Party.

Trump would garner a great deal of attention for his run, though most media outlets tended to discount it as an attempt to build his brand more than a serious bid for the White House. Trump would ultimately decide that the Reform Party could not help him win a national election and withdrew from both the race and the party.

Still, Trump's testing of the waters may have provided the seed which eventually sprouted into his successful bid for the white house in 2016.

Trump's Reality Show Turn

It would be a grievous error to leave out Trump's turn as a reality TV star as being instrumental to his eventual ascen- dency to the White House. In 2004, Trump added a new notch to his belt and listing on his resume – television personality.

With the dawn of the new millennium, television producers began to branch out, looking for different shows to capture the public's attention. With rising competition from the internet and video game consoles, television executives needed to find a "shot in the arm" to get people's eyeballs back on their small screens.

Reality television was born out of an effort to fill this void. The television executives loved the fact that the shows could be produced cheaply. Reality television seemed the perfect solu- tion to their dilemma, with no professional actors or screen- writers to pay and plenty of people lining up for their chance at fifteen seconds of fame.

And it worked. Survivor debuted in 2000 and became one of the most-watched shows in the world. A slew of copycat productions would quickly follow it. Eventually, the idea for *The Apprentice* was cooked up as a way to provide a competitive show without resorting to the big, expensive stunts that defined shows like *Survivor* and *Fear Factor*.

On *The Apprentice,* contestants competed for the chance to work directly under Trump and learn from his keen business acumen. What was initially seen as just another reality show became a global phenomenon, which ran for many seasons before ending in 2017. It should be pointed out the show only ended because of Trump's victory in the 2016 presidential election, not because of low ratings or a lack of interest in the Trump brand by the general public.

The Apprentice introduced Donald Trump to a much wider audience, including a new generation born after his trials and triumphs of the 80s and 90s. The show solidified his public image as a keen, shrewd businessman who had turned a million-dollar loan from his father into a billion-dollar business empire.

The Apprentice would make household names out of

contestants like Omarossa and provided the public with a new view of Trump. Instead of the billionaire playboy image he'd projected for so long, he was now seen as a serious businessman willing to mentor and share his knowledge with a new genera- tion of hopefuls.

One might believe that, given Trump's incredible influence and popularity, he would not have been discounted as a serious candidate for o$ce in 2016. Yet, that's just what happened.

When Trump announced his candidacy in 2015, the general reaction on both sides of the aisle was one of amuse- ment at best or scorn at worst. No one, not even his fellow Republicans, considered him a serious contender for the White House.

Trump entered a decidedly crowded race. The media seemed poised to declare men like Florida Governor Jeb Bush of the famous Bush dynasty the "likely" winner of the Repub- lican nomination. The party and the media gave other candi- dates, like Marco Rubio, more serious attention.

Yet, Trump would not be deterred. He focused on a populist message and made it a point of pride that, unlike his opponents, he was not a career politician. Trump was able to successfully marry the idea of his brand to be a cage-rattling outsider. Someone who would, as he frequently stated, "drain the swamp" in Washington, a referral to corruption.

The media finally began to take Trump seriously, espe- cially as he began polling better than his opponents. The disas- trous invasion of Iraq and Afghanistan had tarnished the Bush legacy, making Jeb's nomination less likely. Not to mention that Jeb was never the most glib of public speakers and had trouble connecting with his audience.

Marco Rubio was seen as an unproven commodity, and his more moderate talking points failed to capture the heart of the electorate in the way that Trump's bombast was able to. Trump was able to tap into a deep thread of resentment and mistrust of the government running through American society. He posi- tioned himself as a Washington outsider with the objectivity and moxie to take on the establishment.

Initially, the Republican establishment seemed reluctant to put Trump forward as its nominee. The establishment felt luke- warm toward the businessman and reality star at best. Still, at the same time, they recognized his ability to connect with voters who sometimes slipped through the cracks of both polit- ical parties.

Thus, the GOP gave Trump a seat at the table, even if they seriously discounted his ability to win either their nomination or the general election to follow. As it turns out, their disdain and doubt only served to fuel Trump's own gumption. The businessman was used to being counted out. People had been counting him out since the 80s, and he had always come out the other side stronger than before.

It quickly became clear that Trump was the most popular nominee for the Republican party. He won his party's nomina- tion and would be put on the ballot against longtime career politician and former First Lady Hillary Rodham Clinton.

Most everyone, even the GOP, figured Trump's victory was a long shot at best. After all, they were facing off against a powerhouse personality and former Secretary of State who had literally grown up in the halls of mighty political power.

Hillary Clinton also had something else that Trump lacked – the unequivocal backing of her own political party, the

Democrats. In fact, it seemed that the Democratic Party went to great lengths to make sure Hillary would be their nominee, utilizing superdelegates and other tactics to keep their own populist candidate, Bernie Sanders, from winning the nomination.

It is unclear how a showdown between Trump and Sanders

would have gone. What is known is how the contest between Clinton and Trump ended.

The Trump campaign was able to capitalize on multiple mistakes on behalf of the Clinton election machine. While Trump appealed to the masses, Clinton was seen as an elitist. She further distanced herself from voters by calling Trump supporters a "basket of deplorables," a sentiment that would haunt her until the end of the campaign.

She also appeared bored and disdainfully amused at her debates with the Manhattan businessman. Meanwhile, Trump stuck to his message and didn't stray from it, garnering more followers as the campaign wore on.

It would be remiss not to mention the possible effect then- FBI director James Comey's investigation into Hillary Clinton had upon the election, seeing as it opened just a few days before election day in 2016. However, while the investigation may have played a small role, it was already obvious that Trump was presenting a far more serious threat than anyone had anticipated. If Clinton were not taking Trump seriously before, she certainly was now.

Trump captured enough of the votes to win a narrow Elec- toral College victory, making him president of the United States. Like George W. Bush in 2000, Trump won the Elec- toral College and lost the popular vote. Given his penchant for maverick disruption, this result was perhaps to be expected.

In spite of seemingly insurmountable odds, Trump had achieved his biggest goal yet – winning the highest office in the United States of America.

CHAPTER 3

TRUMP'S 2016 PRESIDENTIAL CAMPAIGN

"I will be the greatest jobs president that God ever created." ~Presidential Campaign Speech, 2015

WITH TRUMP'S victory in the rearview mirror, many pundits and politicos had the same question: What happened?

How had a man who seemed to court controversy at every turn, with no experience in politics or public office, managed to defeat a solid if a divisive candidate from the opposing party and assume the mantle of president of the United States?

It's not just a harangue, but a legitimate query. In this chapter, we take an in-depth look at how Trump's 2016 presidential campaign was able to sway voters and capture the public imagi- nation in a manner like no other.

Courting Controversy

Most politicians try to walk a delicate balancing act. They struggle to split the difference between appealing to the diehards of their base while also making themselves at least palat- able, if not desirable, of the voters in the "middle" of the aisle.

An excellent example of "splitting the difference" comes courtesy of Bill Clinton during his 1992 presidential campaign. When a reporter asked him if he had ever smoked marijuana, Clinton said yes, he did and then tacked on this now-iconic line: "I didn't inhale."

Clinton was widely criticized for trying to play both sides of the cannabis debate. Yet, in essence, he was going strictly by the politician's playbook. He tried to find common ground between two divergent points and exist there.

However, the public would soon learn that Donald Trump does not play by the standard rules of engagement. Rather, he creates his own rules.

During his lead-up to garnering the Republican nomina- tion, Trump had spouted a great deal of invective rhetoric. Many assumed, including members of his own party, that Trump would now tone down his incendiary speeches and assume a more moderate tone.

As it turned out, they were all wrong.

Trump the candidate was exactly the same as Trump the potential nominee. He saw no reason to change his rhetoric in the least. If it ain't broke, don't fix it, or at least that's how Trump approached his campaign trail.

One of the lighting rod issues which Trump expertly wielded to bring people to his side was immigration, specifi- cally the illegal kind. During a campaign speech, he made one of his more famous quotes:

"In America, we will build a great wall along the southern border. And Mexico will pay for the wall. One hundred percent. They don't know it yet, but they're going to pay for it. And they're great people and great leaders but they're going to pay for the

wall. On day one, we will begin working on intangible (sic), physical, tall, power, beautiful southern border wall."

Trump's wall, as it became to be known, has never been completed, nor has significant construction been done on it. However, while it may have never manifested in a physical sense, the wall is perhaps one of the best examples of Trump being able to wield controversy and hardline stances to his advantage.

It's an irrefutable fact that the US-Mexico border cuts through traditional human migratory paths. This has led to the phenomenon of *illegal* migration, where people from Mexico come north into the United States looking for gainful employ- ment. It should be noted that migration patterns existed since America's discovery and long before.

Trump was able to use the proposed border wall to complete three distinct objectives.

One, he was able to show just how tough he would be in cracking down on illegal immigration. Trump drew his line firmly in the sand and refused to back away from it.

Two, Trump's proposal appealed to his base and made them even stauncher supporters of his campaign and subse- quent policies. The fact that a border wall is impractical and unlikely to stem the worst flow of contraband and illegal immi- grants into the United States—both of which usually come via vehicles that cross the borders legally—was ultimately irrele- vant. It also did not matter that roughly a third of the border was already protected by fences. The wall became symbolic of Trump's hardline textbook Republican policies and helped to solidify his followers into a cohesive whole behind him.

Three, by hawking the virtues of the wall, Trump was able to separate himself from his Democratic rival and make her look soft on illegal immigration. While Hillary Clinton was always more of a right-leaning Democrat than a centrist or hardcore left-winger, Trump's stance on the wall had the effect of making her appear to be a radical leftist who didn't care to protect American interests from the depredations of illegal immigration.

Trump did not limit himself to just rhetoric about building a wall. He also vowed to crack down on people who abused the asylum system and those who overstayed on work visas. Trump was able to successfully marry the idea of higher crime rates and stagnating wages with illegal immigration, though experts agree this correlation is shaky at best.

Trump didn't stop there. He promised to deport all undocumented immigrants and put an end to sanctuary cities, which resisted efforts of immigration control to deport people in the country illegally. Both of these promises were perhaps overly ambitious. For one, finding, detaining, and deporting every undocumented immigrant in the United States was such a daunting task as to be borderline impossible. For another, courts had long sided with sanctuary cities with regard to their policies, making his second promise a difficult one to keep.

None of this mattered one bit to his followers.

To Trump's supporters, his hardline stance against illegal immigration made him the clear candidate of choice over the more moderate politics of Hillary Rodham Clinton. Trump's savvy in manipulating public opinion in his favor was on full display as he enjoyed more support for his policies, impractical though they may have seemed.

One of Trump's more controversial positions during his campaign was to enact a total ban on people of several predomi- nately Muslim faith entering the country on the grounds it would protect Americans from terrorist acts like those perpetu- ated on 9-11. His detractors used this stance as "proof" that Trump was racist and prejudiced against people of the Islamic faith. But the move turned out to be popular among his supporters and ultimately may have helped him secure the White House.

Trump's hardline policies made him unpopular with segments of the population, who considered them discrimina- tory or, at worst, out and out racist. However, none of this both- ered Trump. He had no intention of talking "to the middle" as was the usual playbook for politicians. He intended to stick to his guns and keep them blazing until he'd won the election.

Trade

There is, perhaps, no subject more daunting to handle for any politician than that of international trade. It's a thin high- wire act, and politicians who walk it must be careful. The increasing globalization of trade markets and the rise of cryp- tocurrency made it a murky issue, with little in the way of clear cut right and wrong.

Trump cut through the mire of controversy surrounding the subject of trade and made his stances clear. Once again, he chose to appeal to his populist message rather than towing the Republican party line.

Trump took aim at the TPP, the Trans-Pacific Partnership, in particular, and other trade agreements. The TPP and its ilk had been enacted to help bolster the American economy and make it easier for intentional trade.

However, Trump argued that the TPP and its ilk actually hurt Americans by moving manufacturing jobs out of the country and making wages lower than they needed to be. He promised to withdraw or renegotiate many of these trade deals and get a more favorable outcome for those living in the United States.

Trump also promised to enact stiff Tariffs against countries he saw as taking advantage of the United States, chief among them China. Once again, these policies successfully fired up his base of supporters and increased their loyalty to him. However, many economists from both sides of the aisle warned that such tariffs could have the unintended consequence of making things worse for Americans. Again, the opinion of experts did not cause Trump to lose any followers.

With many Americans feeling left behind by globalization, Trump found an ample foothold in their hearts. He was able to present himself as the champion of the "little guy," similar to how President Nixon positioned himself as the speaker for the so-called silent majority during his own presidency. Once again, Trump turned a negative into a positive and garnered greater support from the electorate than he had enjoyed before.

Healthcare

During the Obama administration, the Democrats champi- oned a plan they eventually turned into the Affordable Care Act or ACA. The ACA, sometimes called Obamacare though Obama's involvement was largely limited to signing the finished bill, proved polarizing for Americans.

While some people benefitted - insurance companies could no longer deny people with pre-existing conditions - overall, the ACA left a bad taste in Americans' mouths. The act had been intended to lower the cost of insurance, but many Americans found themselves paying more for insurance, not less.

Trump took aim at the ACA, one of his more popular moves. He argued that the ACA was a disaster driving up healthcare costs and limiting patient choice. Both of these were valid criticisms, though the problem was more complex than perhaps presented.

Trump proposed a replacement plan that would allow for greater competition among insurance companies, expand the use of health savings accounts, and give states more flexibility in designing their healthcare systems. Trump's replacement plan, however, was criticized for potentially leaving millions of Americans without healthcare coverage.

Whether or not the plan to "repeal and replace" the Affordable Care Act was practical once again did not matter to the voting public. Trump garnered more followers who felt the ACA had negatively impacted their lives.

Taxes

Perhaps no issue stimulates the American consciousness more than the concept of taxes. While most everyone agrees that some taxation is necessary to keep society functional, many believe the tax codes should be rewritten.

Trump expertly tapped into this vein of thought during his campaign in 2016. He proposed lower taxes, arguing that with more money in their pockets, Americans would spend it, thus stimulating the economy.

He also proposed reducing the amount of tax brackets and eliminating the estate tax - two moves that benefited wealthier Americans more than the middle class. However, it has been said that everyone in America is a temporarily embarrassed millionaire, i.e., that they SHOULD be wealthy and have merely suffered a setback. This helps explain why Trump's ideas caught traction even with people in the lowest socio- economic brackets in the country.

Economists once more ventured into the fray, warning that Trump's policies would increase the federal deficit while primarily benefiting the upper socio-economic strata. However, just as before, Trump was able to turn a negative into a positive. He portrayed his detractors as elites out of touch with the average American. Thus their warnings went by and large unheeded, and he gained more voters than he lost as a result of his proposed taxation policies.

National Security

Globalization had made world politics a great deal more complicated. However, national security remained a hot-button issue in the 2016 election. Politicians on both sides of the aisle advocated for stronger national security, even if they had different ideas of how to achieve that goal.

Trump once more tapped into the zeitgeist of the American public's consciousness with his national security policies. Trump also proposed building up and increasing the size of the United States Armed Forces. Trump argued that a stronger military was necessary to protect America in an increasingly unstable global landscape.

Trump promised to pull out all the stops to confront and contain ISIS, also known as the Islamic State of Iraq and Syria. In the wake of the invasion of Iraq and Afghanistan, ISIS had risen above other terrorist organizations like the Taliban to become the most recognizable and powerful of the lot. Many Americans feared ISIS, and Trump knew this and tapped into it to garner support and votes.

Finally, Trump promised to withdraw from a deal forged with Iran where the Muslim-majority country would be permitted to pursue peaceful uses of nuclear energy. He argued that Iran would use the peaceful nuclear program as a smoke- screen to hide the fact they were looking to develop atomic weapons. Again, this tapped into a strong current of agreement with the populist movement.

Ultimately, Trump's policies and promises were a reflection of the deeply divided and polarized state of American politics in 2016 and the large section of the electorate that felt disen- franchised by the government. His successful campaign for president exemplifies this in its essence.

CHAPTER 4

IMMIGRATION

47

"I will build a great, great wall on our southern border, and I will have Mexico pay for that wall. Mark my words." ~ Campaign launch rally, June 15, 2015

DEFYING THE ODDS, conventional wisdom, and even members of his own political party, Donald Trump had done the seemingly impossible.

He had won the 2016 presidential election.

Detractors and supporters alike were forced to prepare for his incoming presidency. Once Trump took the oath of office, many predicted he would "settle down" or at least tone down his policies. However, just like when he won his party's nomination for candidacy, Trump gave no indication of growing more moder- ate. If anything, gaining the highest office in the land seemed to spur Trump on to even more hardline policies than ever before. The Don's campaign promise to secure the U.S. borders and crack down on illegal immigration had been quite popular with Republican voters. However, there have always been exceptions to the general rule that the GOP is anti-immigration.

Two of these exceptions involved groups of immigrants who have traditionally fostered sympathy from the American public, straddling party lines and providing rare common ground.

Refugees and Asylum Seekers

While often used interchangeably, there are legal distinctions between refugees and asylum seekers. Refugees flee their own countries because they are at risk of serious human rights violations and persecution there. The risks to their safety and life were so great that they felt they had no choice but to leave and seek safety outside their country because their own govern- ment could not or would not protect them from those dangers. Refugees have a right to international protection.

By contrast, asylum seekers are people who have left their country and are seeking protection from persecution and serious human rights violations in another country but who hasn't yet been legally recognized as a refugee and is waiting to receive a decision on their asylum claim. Seeking asylum is a human right. This means everyone should be allowed to enter another country to seek asylum.

Refugees and asylum seekers traditionally come from countries where something has made life there untenable or even impossible. Examples would include people affected by natural disasters-earthquakes, typhoons, volcanic eruptions, etc. Many of these disasters destroy key infrastructure and can even make the land itself hostile to human life.

Another factor that can create refugees is economic collapse, which can lead to mass starvation and civil unrest. If daily life becomes untenable in a particular geographic area,

America has traditionally gone out of its way to provide support and succor within its borders.

Refugees were traditionally allowed a great deal of leeway with regard to following normal immigration protocol to the United States on the grounds that it was the humanitarian thing to do. However, Trump's "America First" philosophy caused him to take aim at this traditionally protected group. He made moves to strip refugees of their protections that tradition- ally allowed for easier immigration to the United States.

For example, minors from Central and South America could no longer gain ingress to the United States unless they had a parent or guardian already in the country. Immigrants in the country legally would also find their temporary protected status taken away (Owen, 2019.)

A sad fact of human history is that many new, radical regimes crack down on those they deem as "other." This has been played out all over the world, from Cambodia to the former Yugoslavia territory.

Again the America First philosophy made Trump less sympathetic to asylum seekers. He wanted a more uniform immigration policy and sought to end the protections that tradi- tionally made it easier for asylum seekers to fast-track to citi- zenship.

Trump's hardline stance on refugees and asylum seekers gave fuel to his detractors, who presented it as "proof" that he was heartless and anti-immigrant, legal or not. It would continue to be a hallmark of his presidency until the last days.

Zero-Tolerance and the Separation of Families

Perhaps President Trump's most divisive and outrage- inducing policy of all was his zero-tolerance stance against illegal immigrants.

Formerly, families found trying to cross into the United States illegally were kept together when possible unless their parents were proven to be criminals or if there was a need to remove children from potential predators.

Trump increased the likelihood that children would be taken from their parents during his administration. Children were summarily separated from their families and incarcerated in separate facilities as a standard policy. While Trump

claimed this was for security's sake, the move may have ultimately caused him more political harm than good.

When the policy was enacted in 2018, there was a massive public outcry. Republicans and Democrats alike were horrified by the footage coming out of ICE detention facilities, which depicted children as young as three in jail cells. "No Kids in Cages" became a popular refrain for people opposed to this family separation policy.

Trump's GOP colleagues sought to distance themselves from the president and his policies, though Attorney General Jeff Sessions made an attempt to justify the policy. Unfortu- nately, Sessions-who would ultimately be fired by President Trump - chose to use a Bible verse to justify the policy.

Besides raising the ire of those who support a strong separation of church and state, Sessions' quote was also a favorite of slaveowners in the deep south before and during the Civil War. *"Romans 13, to obey the laws of the government because*

God has ordained the government for his purposes."

Some of Trump's own cabinet sought to deny the policy even existed. Homeland Security Secretary Kristjen Neilson said, "We do not have a policy of separating families at the border, period."

Unfortunately, she was soon confronted by a missive from Attorney General Jeff Sessions outlining the policy in detail. Her sudden reversal was seen as hypocrisy writ large in the eyes of many. However, Trump managed to avoid the worst of the fallout of this unpopular policy.

The family separation policy would eventually end, but not before almost three thousand children had been detained and separated from their families. The images of young children being kept in cages would haunt Trump until the end of his presidency in 2021.

Build the Wall

Call it an untenable, unpractical policy, or call it a stroke of genius politicking. In either case, the Build the Wall movement became synonymous with Trump and his unique brand of political discourse.

Donald Trump expertly generated a tremendous amount of political momentum via his plan to build the wall. A border wall with Mexico had often been a talking point on conservative media outlets, but no other Republican politi- cians had been as vociferous in pushing the idea before Trump.

Donald Trump didn't want to fall into the same trap that his predecessors had post-election. During the 1988 presiden- tial election, for example, George H.W. Bush went on the record with his proposed tax plan.

"Read my lips. No new taxes."

Facing an unexpectedly tough challenge from Democratic rival Michael Dukakis, Bush needed to reassure the American people that he would not raise their taxes. This became espe- cially poignant after Dukakis promised to raise taxes as a "last resort."

The plan worked perfectly. Bush defeated his nemesis and assumed the mantle of the president of the United States of America. The voting public was more than willing to put their faith in the candidate who guaranteed they would not raise taxes.

But the senior Bush soon faced a problem upon taking office. His predecessor in the White House, Ronald Reagan, had enacted policies that led to severe budget crises on multiple fronts. George Bush even called Reagan's plans "voodoo economics" while the two debated for the Republican nomina- tion in 1980.

It became clear that Bush's position was untenable (Roth-man, 2018.) He was forced to backtrack his proposal, which led to his ridicule on late-night talk shows and *Saturday Night Live*

in particular, where comedian Dana Carvey would repeat the "read my lips" line in a variety of outlandish scenarios.

With this image clearly in mind, Donald Trump set out to keep his campaign promise. Unfortunately, his outsider status, which had helped propel him to the White House, became a hindrance. Used to calling all of the shots in his own business empire, Trump now learned that Washington D.C. played by much different rules.

Trump soon found that he had no way to coerce Mexico

into paying for his border wall, as he had promised on the campaign trail. But the Don remained undaunted and began to examine other avenues to secure funding.

In a shrewd bit of politicking, Trump was able to declare the situation at the US-Mexico border to be a crisis situation.

This allowed him to appropriate $2.5 billion from the national defense budget to use in construction of the wall.

Democrats in Congress wasted no time in raising a legal challenge against the wall. They were joined in their efforts by environmental groups and the American Civil Liberties Union. These groups argued that the Trump administration had violated the Constitution by going around Congress using a

bogus emergency declaration.

Several court rulings went against the administration until the case reached the Supreme Court. The Supreme Court ruled in a 5-4 decision, split between party lines that the construction could continue while the Trump Administration appealed the lower court decisions (Alvarez, 2020.)

In the end, Trump's wall is best viewed as a partial success. While he did manage to get over four hundred miles of it built, only around 70 miles were built in areas that did not already have existing border barriers in place (Hansen, 2022.) While Trump tried his utmost to fulfill his campaign promise, the American political system and its checks and balances on Exec- utive branch power would ultimately prevent the wall's completion.

Stay in Mexico

The Trump Administration adopted a hairline, controver- sial stance against immigration. It was called the Stay in Mexico policy.

The administration said the policy was necessary to combat crime, which he linked to illegal immigration. Critics claimed the policy to be inhumane and racist. However, Trump was still able to exert a lot of influence and slow the flow of immigrants across the US's southern border.

Banning Immigration from Muslim Countries.

Donald Trump signed an executive order on January 27, 2017, to ban foreign nationals from seven predominantly Muslim countries from visiting the country for 90 days, suspend entry to the country of all Syrian refugees indefinitely, and prohibit any other refugees from entering the country for 120 days.

The move proved controversial, but the Don has never been afraid to push boundaries. Immediately, immigrant rights groups and the American Civil Liberties Union filed lawsuits to challenge the executive order.

Trump's orders would be ruled against by several courts and eventually blocked by a federal judge just twelve days after being issued.

Undaunted, Trump would try two more versions of the executive order, each one more moderate than the last. The Supreme Court would rule in favor of Trump's third Muslim ban, watered down though it was, in another 5-4 decision (McGraw, 2017).

The ban would eventually be buried under the more pressing concerns of the worldwide pandemic and eventually expired. However, the ban should be considered a success of Trump's administration, as they were able to achieve their goal, albeit temporarily.

The Fight to End DACA

The DACA program, or Deferred Action for Childhood Arrivals, was created by the Obama administration to aid people brought to the country illegally as children by their parents or guardians.

The beneficiaries of the program became popularly known as Dreamers. Trump took aim at the DACA program in 2017, looking to rescind it "immediately."

Attorney General Jeff Sessions announced in a press conference that the DACA program would be phased out, affecting nearly three-quarters of a million people in the United States. Trump attempted to work with a bipartisan congressional committee to find a compromise, but his fiery rhetoric soon drew the ire of the Democrats on the committee.

Trump allegedly stated, "Why are we having all of these people from s**thole countries coming here?"

While the meetings were, by and large, closed sessions, Senator Dick Durbin of Illinois made Trump's comments public. Trump reacted by ending bipartisan negotiations and claiming that Durbin had harmed the country and ended DACA.

Thanks to a government shutdown, Democrats were able to successfully attach a provision that stated the Senate would "immediately proceed" to consider Daca-related legislation upon returning to work (Savage, 2019).

DACA might be one of Trump's lasting legacies. As of this writing, a federal judge has found the program to be "unlaw- ful" but has allowed it to continue for those already enrolled in it. The Biden administration is appealing the decision, but for

now, it looks like Trump has successfully terminated the program for all intents and purposes.

Donald Trump has seen many of his immigration initiatives challenged, delayed, or even reversed. However, there is no denying his indelible imprint upon U.S. immigration, and the effects will no doubt last for many years to come.

CHAPTER 5

MAKING AMERICA GREAT

THE COMEBACK KING: DONALD TRUMP'S UNFINISHED BUSINESS

"The line of 'Make America great again,' the phrase, that was mine, I came up with it about a year ago, and I kept using it, and everybody's using it, they are all loving it. I don't know, I guess I should copyright it, maybe I have copyrighted it." ~ MyFox New York, March 2015

NEVER HAS SUCH a phrase proved more controversial or divisive, nor used at a 'litmus test' for a personality like Make America Great Again.

Frequently presented as the acronym MAGA, the phrase has graced hats, t-shirts, social media cover pages, and numerous other media in the years before, during, and after Trump's presidency.

While Trump did not coin the phrase-the credit for that goes to former president Ronald Reagan-he certainly took it to a new height of popularity. (Margelin, 2016.)

Donald Trump had ambitions beyond selling t-shirts and coffee mugs, however. He wanted to make the Make America

Great Again slogan into more than just a catchphrase. He wanted it to reflect reality.

To that end, he made revitalizing the manufacturing industry in the United States a top priority. Indeed, when Trump campaigned, he frequently stated his desire to bring jobs back to the United States and reduce the trade deficit with foreign countries.

In order to make his dream a reality, Trump eschewed working with Congress and instead signed an executive order called "Buy American, Hire American." The main impetus of the order could almost be considered another facet of Trump's immigration policy since the main tenets involved pressuring

U.S. companies that hired foreign labor.

Unfortunately, the order proved difficult to implement for the understaffed labor department. Critics lambasted the exec- utive order as simplistic and unrealistic, though some in the manufacturing sector hailed it as a stride in the right direction (Hamlin, 2017).

Withdrawing from the Trans-Pacific Partnership

The TPP was pushed hard by the Obama administration. In a nutshell, the deal was for eleven Pacific bordering coun- tries in North and South America to smooth out and reduce the costs of trade among themselves.

The hope was that the TPP would continue to allow the

U.S. to dominate the Asian export market and increase prof- itability for U.S. companies.

Trump was opposed to the TPP on the grounds that the companies who benefitted had no legal obligation to turn their new windfall into increased jobs or wages. His incendiary rhetoric, which involved likening the TPP to "rape" caused a lot of controversies. However, few on either side of the aisle truly liked the act.

Trump signed an executive order withdrawing the U.S. from the TPP on January 23, 2017. While many were glad to see the TPP in the rearview mirror, there were critics who feared Trump might trigger a trade war (Popken, 2017).

After the repeal of the TPP, Trump would focus on making separate trade deals with individual nations involved in the original pact.

Trump and the USMCA

Since the 1990s, U.S. trade has operated under the auspices of the North American Free Trade Act, or NAFTA for short.

NAFTA was similar in many respects to the TPP in that its goal was to ensure U.S.market dominance in trade throughout North America. The deal involved the USA, Canada, and Mexico.

NAFTA was never a terribly popular entity on either side of the aisle, but it remained in effect nonetheless. That is until Trump was able to successfully replace it with a successor: the United States-Canada-Mexico Agreement (USMCA).

Even though it was meant to replace NAFTA, USMCA kept many key provisions from the original. However, it also provided a new, updated groundwork for dealing with issues not present or significant in the 1990s. Chief among these were intellectual property, or IP, and issues pertaining to the inter- net, which had become ubiquitous with modern life.

The USMCA prioritized automobile manufacturing in the US. As a boost to dairy farmers, the USMCA also allowed U.S. farmers to sell their produce to Canadian businesses.

In addition, the USMCA provided tougher labor laws in

Mexico and reduced the protections drug manufacturers had enjoyed under NAFTA.

Unlike most of Trump's policies, many of which were repealed or proved difficult to implement, the USMCA stands out as an unmitigated triumph (Swansen-Tankersly, 2020).

The Global Pandemic

COVID-19 took the world by storm, proving one of the most infectious and communicable viruses in modern history. While not as deadly as other viruses, such as Ebola, COVID was easily transferrable between people and had debilitating, long and short-term consequences for those infected.

The pandemic would disrupt businesses and supply chains all around the world. Trump's response to the pandemic was criticized by many.

Firstly, and perhaps most damaging to the Don's reputa- tion, was the fact he had disbanded the NSC Pandemic Response team.

The National Security Council Pandemic response team's main purpose was to combat the spread of infectious diseases like COVID. By having the team assembled and ready to go, it was hoped that the NSC could get ahead of pandemics before they could do irreparable harm.

Trump believed having a permanent staff was financially wasteful, so long as no pandemics were raging. Disbanding the team definitely contributed to the haphazard way in which the crisis was handled (Reichmann, 2020).

In addition to disbanding the team, President Trump didn't declare a state of emergency until after the pandemic had been raging for months. Even then, he refused to issue a national lockdown order, preferring to leave that matter to individual state governments.

Donald Trump would take to his favorite medium-Twitter-to voice his displeasure with the criticism his pandemic response received. He sent the following tweet on March 11, 2020:

"The Media should view this as a time of unity and strength. We have a common enemy, actually, an enemy of the World, the CoronaVirus. We must beat it as quickly and safely as possible. There is nothing more important to me than the life & safety of the United States!"

Trump was also politically savvy enough to use the

pandemic to help justify his border policy. He sent the following tweet on March 13, 2020:

"To this point, and because we have had a very strong border policy, we have had 40 deaths related to CoronaVirus. If we had weak or open borders, that number would be many times higher!"

Trump's administration made a policy out of minimizing

the threat the virus presented and maximizing the PR of their own efforts to combat it. However, the virus proved how infec- tious it was by infecting the president himself.

On October 3, 2020, the president was forced to abandon his campaign trail and enter the hospital. He had succumbed to the virus and required supplemental oxygen on the third and fourth day of that month (Aljazeera, 2020).

The president would be out of the hospital by October 8th
and back on the campaign trail. Even Trump's recovery from
a deadly disease was criticized by many, who said he had
access to better care than the rest of the country did.

However, many also praised Trump for quickly entering
medical treatment and wearing a mask to protect others
from infection.

In the end, it's hard to say how differently things might have
unfolded if Trump had not been our pandemic president.

Many of the difficulties encountered, such as the disruption in supply chains and economic downturn, would have happened no matter who was in the White House. One thing is certain - Trump's legacy on coronavirus leaves people and opinions as divided as almost anything else pertaining to the polarizing Don.

MAGA Conclusion

Donald Trump's sincere efforts to Make America Great Again proved as controversial and divisive as the man himself.

On the one hand, he did carry out some of his campaign promises. On the other, his handling of the pandemic and the resulting fallout was heavily criticized. Objectively, the ques- tion must be asked whether America is better or worse off thanks to the MAGA initiative.

However, it is a question without a clear-cut or definite answer. The results of Trump's MAGA policy were very much a mixed bag. While his base of supporters remained as ardent as ever, Trump also failed to convince the middle or the left of the efficacy of his programs, executive orders, and general philosophy.

Looking ahead, it seems as if Trump's legacy of making America great again is checkered, though the USMC pact remains a solid success story for the Don.

CHAPTER 6

MONETARY POLICY

THE COMEBACK KING: DONALD TRUMP'S UNFINISHED BUSINESS

"My only question is, who is the greater enemy Jay Powell or XiPing" ~
Twitter

THE QUESTION of what is best for the economy is a tricky one at best. If managing the marketplace were simple, there would not be a long history of ups and downs, booms and crashes.

As a billionaire businessman, Donald Trump seemed more than qualified to navigate the murky waters of the U.S. stock market and financial systems. Many of his supporters pointed to this aspect of his character as being an ideal qualification to hold the office of the presidency.

However, as president, Trump would soon learn that his words carried much greater weight than they did when he was a private businessman. It didn't matter if those words were spoken, written, or in one particular case, tweeted.

...

The Tweets That Crashed the Markets

Twitter began its life exemplifying the Shakespearian tenet "brevity is the soul of wit." By limiting the amount of characters users could use on a single post or tweet, as the website dubbed them, the company hoped to refine discourse and deal with the ever-shrinking attention span of humanity.

Donald Trump soon settled upon Twitter as his preferred medium for addressing the nation. There were positives and negatives about this fact. On the positive side, it allowed for a much greater reach for his words. People who did not have the time or opportunity to watch press conferences on standard television broadcasts could take a quick minute to check their phones and catch up on what the president was up to.

On the negative side, Twitter's huge reach became a down- fall because the things President Trump tweeted about would often have unintended consequences. It was apparent nowhere more readily than when Trump's tweets caused a major fall in the stock markets.

It all began, as many of Trump's policies, with the best of intentions. Trump believed that by raising tariffs on foreign imports, he could protect the U.S.dollar and American jobs. However, his tweets on May 5, 2019, achieved much the opposite. *For 10 months, China has been paying Tari!s to the USA of 25% on 50 Billion Dollars of High Tech, and 10% on 200 Billion Dollars of other goods. These payments are partially responsible for our great economic results. The 10% will go up to*

25% on Friday. 325 Billions Dollars....
....of additional goods sent toU.S.by China remain untaxed, but will be shortly, at a rate of 25%. The Tari!s paid to the USA have had little impact on product cost, mostly borne by China. The Trade Deal with China continues, but too slowly, as they attempt to renegotiate. No!

The two-part tweet would become known in financial circles as "The 102 words that erased about $1.36 trillion from global stocks."

The fears of an impending trade war combined with the already volatile COVID-plagued market proved too much for the stock exchanges worldwide. Not only did they spark losses, but volatility came roaring back with a vengeance, with the Cboe Volatility Index rising 50 percent in two days to breach 20 (Baligi-Burgress, 2019).

The way a tariff works is that it's basically like a sales tax, except instead of being paid on all goods, it's paid only on imported goods. A tax on Chinese-made goods is obviously bad

for Chinese manufacturers. But as with any kind of tax, the financial price is largely paid by consumers of Chinese-made goods — and, critically, by consumers of domestic goods that compete with Chinese-made ones (Yglesas, 2019).

Donald Trump had hoped to bolster the U.S. economy by enforcing stricter tariffs against China. However, his efforts led to a trade war that hindered the economy rather than bolstering it. Trump's tariff tweets proved two things. One, that the global economy was more complex than the New York real estate market. Two, the president's words carried heavy weight and could lead to grave consequences.

Taking on the Federal Reserve

Donald Trump was not the first critic of the Federal Reserve. In fact, the Fed, as it is often called, has been the target of criticism almost since its inception.

The Federal Reserve was formed to fulfill several functions for the United States. It is often referred to as the central bank of the United States. The Fed manages inflation, regulates the national banking system, stabilizes financial markets, protects consumers, and more.

Although the president appoints the Fed board members, it is designed to function independently of political influence. This allows it a great deal of leeway but also makes it the target of frequent criticism by political entities on both sides of the aisle.

The Fed plays a significant role in financial concerns that affect the lives of all Americans, even if they don't directly invest in the stock market, own property, or have a great deal of savings.

One of the main functions of the Federal Reserve regards setting interest rates for loans. This seemingly simple task has myriad effects on the American financial systems.

Perhaps the most influential chairman of the Federal Reserve was Alan Greenspan. His tenure lasted beyond presi- dential terms and even changing political parties. He served from 1988 until 2007 at his post. His most successful period was the 1990s, when unemployment reached a low of 4%, and inflation was almost stagnant.

However, Greenspan's loose policies have been accused of causing the financial crisis of 2008, and the Fed's reputation has been steadily on the decline ever since (Thomas, 2015),

After announcing his candidacy for president, Trump accused the Fed of keeping interest rates low to help Obama's mercurial approval ratings. It was just the opening salvo against the institution by the Don.

In 2018, the Federal Reserve raised interest rates several times. The Fed claimed these steps were necessary to prevent inflation and keep the economy stable. However, President Trump took major issue with this.

I'm not thrilled because, you know, we go up. And every

time you go up, they want to raise rates again. And I don't really

- I am not happy about it. ~ CNBC interview, 2018.

Trump's position didn't necessarily contradict those on the left side of the political spectrum who also believed raising the interest rates was unnecessary (Zarolli, 2018).

However, Trump broke with a long-standing tradition, though not a rule, on presidents not commenting publicly about the Federal Reserve's policies. As usual, Maverick Trump was undaunted, as his comments later in the interview illustrate.

"Somebody would say, oh, maybe you shouldn't say that as a president. I couldn't care less what they say because my views haven't changed. I don't like - all of this work that we're putting into the economy, and then I see rates going up."

Trump's words would cause a slight dip in the markets, though not as dramatic as his tweets about China tariffs. (Zarolli, 2018.) In the same interview, the Don stressed that he respected the Fed's political independence and would not seek to change its policy directly.

However, Trump would continue his criticism of the Federal Reserve on Twitter.

"The Fed Rate, over a fairly short period of time, should be reduced by at least 100 basis points, with perhaps some quantitative easing as well. If that happened, our Economy would

be even better, and the World Economy would be greatly and quickly enhanced — good for everyone."

Trump would even go so far as to criticize the man he appointed personally to be chairman of the Federal Reserve, Jerome Powell. He called Powell a "stubborn child" who was doing a "bad job."

Many saw Trump's comments and tweets as an attack on the independence of the Federal Reserve itself. This, of course, did nothing to hinder the Don's loquacious criticisms.

...

Tax Cuts and Jobs Act of 2017

One of President Donald Trump's biggest legislative wins came via the Tax Cuts and Jobs Act (TCJA) of 2017.

The act's biggest impetus was lowering the corporate tax rate from 35% to 21%. It also doubled the deduction amounts for most Americans. While this did lead to a greater national deficit, Trump argued it was necessary to stimulate the economy and provide job growth while curbing inflation.

The effects of the tax cuts are difficult to understand, partly because of so many other factors going on in America during their implementation. Trump's trade war with China, his row with the Federal Reserve, and the COVID pandemic all served to obfuscate the picture.

However, it is generally agreed upon by financial experts that the TCJA disproportionately favored wealthier Americans and corporations. Most American taxpayers saw an average increase of about $90 in their tax returns. But those who made above $200,000 per year saw much higher returns (Silva, 2021).

Weakening the Frank-Dodd Act of 2010

In 2010, America was reeling from the worst recession since the Great Depression. In order to combat this, Congress passed the Frank-Dodd Act. This legislation proved both sweeping and historic. One of its major provisions was desig- nating any bank with more than $50 billion in assets a "systemi- cally important" financial institution - or "too big to fail" - and thus subject to enhanced prudential standards, such as "stress tests" and certain capital planning and liquidity requirements.

Dodd-Frank massively empowered the Federal Reserve to more forcefully regulate banks, including those where it wasn't the direct bank regulator (Hutzlter, 2023).

Trump managed to get legislation passed that some say gutted the protections provided by the Frank-Dodd Act.

There were many changes in the legislation. Among them was raising the asset threshold for "systemically important" institutions from $50 billion to $250 billion. Under the law, the Federal Reserve still had the right to apply the Dodd-Frank regulations to banks with at least $100 billion in assets if they chose to do so, however.

Trump signed it into law in May 2018. The Don would call it a "big deal for our country." The push to alter Dodd-Frank split the Democratic Party, and ultimately more than a dozen Senate Democrats joined Republicans to support the deregulations, making it at least in part a bipartisan affair.

"It reduced stress testing, it reduced collateral calculations, it reduced the supervisory stress test and it enabled them not to publicly conduct or report their own company-run stress tests," Dennis Kelleher, the president and CEO of the nonprofit Better Markets, said of the 2018 law. "It blew a hole in several of the key financial stability protection rules."

At first, the effects of weakening regulations could not be felt, as is typical with such legislation. However, the recent, as of this writing, collapse of the Silicon Valley Bank has been tied directly to the massive deregulation included in the 2018 legislation.

Silicon Valley Bank, a regional lender with $210 billion in assets, served the tech industry for 40 years. It collapsed in

two days, marking the largest bank failure since the 2008
financial crisis.

Two days after that came the fall of Signature Bank, the
nation's 29th-largest bank, suggesting that the banking crisis
had spread (\ahn, 2023).

Deregulation is often praised by banks and decried by
economists. The threshold for what is too big to fail would

seem more fluid and less static than believed by the Trump administration.

Overall, Trump's monetary policy was marked by contro- versy and uncertainty. While he made some efforts to stimulate economic growth and reduce taxes for businesses, his criticisms of the Federal Reserve and his imposition of tariffs had a nega- tive impact on the U.S. economy.

His weakening of banking regulations would seem to have caused, at least in part, the collapse of SVB and Signature Bank. Thus, his legacy on monetary reform is a checkered one when viewed objectively through the lens of time.

However, it should be noted that the COVID pandemic greatly impacted the economy as well, leading to job losses and supply chain issues. Without the pandemic, it's unclear what effect Trump's monetary policies might have had had they existed in a virus-free vacuum.

CHAPTER 7

POLITICS

THE COMEBACK KING: DONALD TRUMP'S UNFINISHED BUSINESS

"I'm the most successful person ever to run for the presi- dency, by far. Nobody's ever been more successful than me. I'm the most successful person ever to run. Ross Perot isn't successful like me. Romney - I have a Gucci store that's worth more than Romney." ~ Des Moines Regis- ter, June 2, 2015

WHEN IT COMES TO POLITICS, Donald Trump has proven to be every bit the maverick he was in all other aspects of his life.

While Trump campaigned for, and eventually won, the Republican nomination in 2016, his political views have never been strictly dictated by conservative mores. The best thing to be said about his politicking is that he does it his own way, like everything else.

Most political candidates position themselves to appear with a certain amount of humility. They are, after all, campaigning for a job that is considered a civil service position.

Donald Trump chose to do the exact opposite, as the quote at the start of this chapter attests.

The Don has always been known as a disruptor of the status quo, though only history will be able to truly judge if that is for good or ill. Donald Trump, on his path to the presidency, presented himself as the most successful person to ever run for the office.

Whether or not Trump was truly the most successful indi-vidual to run for president of the United States is up for debate. However, Trump is, without a shadow of a doubt, the most *famous* person to ever run for the office.

Trump expertly parlayed his reality show fame into polit- ical clout. Many people who had been turned off by the Amer- ican political system, those who felt disenfranchised or disgusted by the perceived corruption, were willing to take a chance on the star of *The Apprentice.*

Trump's approach to politics was both unconventional and a game-changer. Typically, politicians tended to take a balanced, sometimes even vague, approach to where they stood on the issues at hand. Trump not only took stands, but he also drew lines in the sand and dared others to cross them.

His approach, while undeniably successful in the 2016 presidential race, has been met with criticism. Some believe that his approach eroded democratic norms and further polar- ized America into an "us versus them" policy.

Border and Immigration Policy

As discussed previously, Trump's hardline stance on immi- gration and border security was a hallmark of his campaign and eventual presidency.

Many politicians, especially those from southern border states, have adopted or tried to adopt similar policies with regard to immigration, such as Greg Abbot from Texas or Arkansas' Asa Hutchinson.

However, those politicians refrained from the kind of inflammatory rhetoric that characterized The Don's swaggering persona. In 2016, he made the following statement while on the campaign trail.

"When Mexico sends its people, they're not sending their best. They're not sending you. They're not sending you. They're sending people that have lots of problems, and they're bringing those problems with us. They're bringing drugs. They're bringing crime. They're rapists. And some, I assume, are good people."

Trump's comments went over well with the Republican base, but more moderate conservatives and the left were horrified at his blatant accusations. While he did add on the caveat at the end that he assumed some of the immigrants were good people, it was the overt negativity that would continue to haunt him throughout his presidency and beyond.

Donald Trump's immigration and border policy will always be one of his biggest legacies, though only history will judge if it is a positive or a negative one he leaves behind.

What's clear is that most candidates, after having uttered an inflammatory statement like the one above, could have kissed their political careers goodbye.

But not in the case of the Comeback King.

Economic Policies

As previously discussed in the monetary policy chapter, Donald Trump made economic reform one of his top priorities. Naturally, this matter was politicized with great aplomb by the Don.

It seems almost a daily occurrence that, somewhere in

America, a factory is shutting down, or a major company is shunting jobs overseas. Every one of those stories has hundreds, sometimes thousands, of individuals attached to it. Individuals who have lost income, careers, homes, and even their lives over the ever-shifting sphere of financial ups and downs.

Trump's political agenda of keeping jobs in America and eliminating trade deficits thus found a ready audience who felt that both parties had let them down for decades. Trump was able to garner support from people who are often considered apolitical, which greatly increased his influence.

Donald Trump also promised to withdraw America from the widely unpopular North American Free Trade Agreement. Trump's successful replacement of NAFTA with the USMCA agreement will forever go down as one of his greatest achieve- ments while holding the office of president.

His supporters saw this as proof that he really did have their interests at heart. Though many of Trump's economic reforms backfired, there is no doubt he was able to fully capi- talize on them for political gain, successful or not. The Don's emphasis on more American manufacturing also increased his political clout, gaining the support of a large swath of the working class.

America First

Perhaps no other phrase has been more polarizing and controversial than Trump's America First policy.

While everyone generally agrees policies that favor Amer- ican companies and citizens aren't a bad thing, critics worried about the similarity to Trump's phrasing and that used by the white nationalist group The America First Committee of 1940 during the build-up to World War II.

The America First Committee argued that American intervention in the Second World War was not only unnecessary but also potentially harmful. They encouraged turning a blind eye to Hitler's atrocities. The connotations of the phrase can't be understated in a modern sense (Diamond, 2018).

Donald Trump ignored the critics, as was his idiom. He continued to use the phrase America First when describing his policies. He made this clear when he withdrew from the Paris Climate Agreement in 2020.

During his campaign and, later, during his presidency, Donald Trump made it clear he wanted an energy production boom in the United States. In particular, he wanted to revi- talize the coal industry, which had been hit hard by a variety of factors, including stricter environmental protection laws.

The USA represents a whopping 15% of greenhouse gas emissions globally, so its withdrawal from the agreement was viewed with suspicion at best, and outright hostility at worst. Trump, however, argued that other major greenhouse gas contributors, China and India, would not be under the same restrictions on burning fossil fuels as the United States, so the withdrawal was necessary to keep the country competitive. (McGrath, 2020.)

Donald Trump also withdrew from a deal struck with Iran over its peaceful use of nuclear energy as part of his America First policy. In a brief, eleven-minute press conference from the White House in 2018, he said the following:

THE COMEBACK KING: DONALD TRUMP'S UNFINISHED BUSINESS

"The Iran deal is defective at its core. If we do nothing, we know exactly what will happen. In just a short period of time the world's leading state sponsor of terror will be on the cusp of acquiring the world's most dangerous weapon. Therefore I am announcing today that the United States will withdraw from the Iran nuclear deal."

Trump's claims of Iran being the "world's leading state sponsor of Terror" are difficult to prove at best, but he would go on to make good on his promise to withdraw from the agree- ment and apply strict sanctions to Iran-sanctions that had been waived in the face of the Obama-era negotiations (Berenson, 2018).

Diverging from the Republican Party Line

There were two key areas where Donald Trump ran against his own political party.

One, he was in favor of paid maternity leave for workers. His daughter Ivanka was a key influence on The Don in his pursuit of this goal. Trump promised on the campaign trail to deliver twelve weeks of paid maternity leave.

Under the Family Medical Leave Act of 1993, workers were only guaranteed unpaid leave. Like many of his campaign promises, however, Trump found that providing paid leave was much harder than he anticipated.

In the end, Donald Trump was able to deliver on his campaign promise, though it would only apply to federal workers (Jacobson, 2020).

Another key area Trump differed from his fellow Republi- cans was on infrastructure repair. With a great deal of bridges, highways, sewers, and other public works systems in shambles after years of neglect, the Don saw it as a problem that crossed party lines.

Trump presented his infrastructure plan to Congress in February of 2018, with a promise of $200 billion in investment in America's infrastructure. This put him at odds with many Senate and House Republicans, who believed state and local governments should fundraise for infrastructure repair on their own.

While Trump did indeed get his infrastructure plan off the ground, there are numerous indications it was not as successful as he might have hoped. Federal funds were hard to come by, especially for urban areas. Congress was forced to act and cap the spending on rural infrastructure funding because of the imbalance (Bliss, 2020).

Shift to Conservatism

During the early 2000s, The Don focused mainly on his business empire, real estate, and of course, his starring role on the reality show hit *The Apprentice*.

However, as the decade wore on, he began to drift toward more conservative viewpoints. One of his more controversial stances had to do with the "birther" movement, a widely- debunked theory that Barack Obama was not born in the United States and was, therefore, ineligible to hold the office of president.

Trump would also begin a tour of the conservative talk show circuit, where he espoused his birther ideas and hinted at a run for the White House himself.

Politics Conclusion

Trump's politics were controversial but also undeniably influential. His reliance on bombast and rhetoric, as well as hardline stances, have been echoed by other members of the Republican party, such as Marjorie Taylor-Greene, and Ron DeSantis.

While his politics were divisive, they did change how many political campaigns are run.

CHAPTER 8

DOMESTIC POLICY

CATHERINE MCCARTHY

"I think if this country gets any kinder or gentler, it's literally going to cease to exist." ~ Playboy, March 1990

THE COMEBACK KING: DONALD TRUMP'S UNFINISHED BUSINESS

DONALD TRUMP'S America First policy was a central theme of his presidency, focusing on putting the interests of the United States before those of other countries. The policy was seen as a departure from traditional U.S. foreign policy, which has been focused on maintaining international alliances and promoting global cooperation.

The Move Against Globalization

Starting as early as the post-war 1950s but really gaining steam in the 1990s, the concept of globalization has always been a polarizing one. The core philosophy of globalization is that all human beings live on the same planet; and the effects of one country's policies don't necessarily stop at their own borders.

While many hail globalization as the natural evolution of human society, there are other voices who have always spoken against it. By and large, these voices tend to come from the right side of the aisle. Most of the criticisms are levied against the idea that globalization is more about being pro-capital than pro- free trade.

Trump's America First policy could be seen as globaliza- tion in reverse (Rogers, 2017). Rather than seeking cooperation for mutual benefit, the Don saw an opportunity to negotiate deals that blatantly favored American businesses and interests.

While his base applauded, many were concerned about the unintended side e$ects of his policies. They thought that it could lead to the U.S. engaging in extreme isolationism - the same type that allowed numerous atrocities to occur during various periods of history, most especially during the Second World War.

There was also a belief that the anti-globalization stance would weaken international relations and create global instabil- ity. Like many of Trump's policies, his stance would make his followers more ardent but fail to swell their number.

Trade and Tariffs

As covered in the monetary policy chapter, one of Trump's
major goals was to reduce the trade deficit with other
countries. He believed that many trade policies and
negotiated deals were detrimental to America's prosperity.
Trump's political savvy made him quick to attach real world
stakes to his policy, as he stated in 2018.

*"I have visited the laid o! factory workers and the communi-
ties crushed by our horrible and unfair trade deals. These are
the*

forgotten men and women of our country and they are forgotten, but they're not gonna be forgotten long. These are people who work hard but no longer have a voice. I am your voice!"

Once again, the Comeback King was able to tap into a vein of disenfranchised Americans who provided a ready audience for his ideals.

Trump's major target for reducing the trade deficit was China. He worked vigorously to put tariffs on Chinese goods into place. His goal was to force U.S. companies to buy Amer- ican and build American.

Unfortunately, his good intentions did not meet with fruition. According to the Commerce Department, the trade deficit soared under the Trump administration (Palmer 2021). When forced to eschew business with China, U.S. companies turned to other foreign countries rather than domestic sources.

Mistrust of International Organizations

Donald Trump's America First policy was at odds with the very idea of international organizations like the United Nations.

A globalist idea from its inception, the United Nations was founded after World War II in the hopes that the horrors of genocide and war could be avoided in the future through mutual cooperation. However, as numerous historical examples will illustrate, the UN has a checkered record at best with stop- ping these phenomena.

Donald Trump railed against the UN several times. He made it clear he did not feel the UN was worth the investment. He made the following remarks at lunch with U.N. Security Council Ambassadors on April 24, 2017.

"The United States, just one of 193 countries in the U.N.,

pays for 22 percent of the budget and almost 30 percent of the United Nations peacekeeping, which is unfair."

It would not be the only time that the Don would attack the UN. He made the following comments at the American Israel Public Affairs Committee speech on March 21, 2016:

"Which brings me to my next point, the utter weakness and

incompetence of the United Nations. The United Nations is not a friend of democracy, it's not a friend to freedom, it's not a friend even to the United States of America where, as you know, it has its home. And it surely is not a friend to Israel."

Trump not only displayed mistrust of the UN, he also sowed it among his followers. It seemed like nothing was off limits for the Don. He even criticized the interior design of the UN building itself in the following tweet on Oct. 3, 2012:

"The cheap 12 inch sq. marble tiles behind speaker at UN always bothered me. I will replace with beautiful large marble slabs if they ask me."

The United Nations would not be the only international organization that Trump would show mistrust of. He also spoke at great length about America's involvement in the North Atlantic Treaty Organization. NATO had been seen as a cornerstone of America's security plans since the end of the Second World War. However, Trump repeatedly expressed his discontent with the organization. He said the following in a 2016 interview with the *New York Times'* editorial board:

CATHERINE MCCARTHY

"I'll tell you the problems I have with NATO. Number one, we pay far too much. We are spending — you know, in fact, they're even making it so the percentages are greater. NATO is unfair, economically, to us, to the United States. Because it really helps them more so than the United States, and we pay a dispro- portionate share. Now, I'm a person that — you notice I talk about economics quite a bit, in these military situations, because it is about economics, because we don't have money anymore

because we've been taking care of so many people in so many di!erent forms that we don't have money — and countries, and countries. So NATO is something that at the time was excellent. Today, it has to be changed. It has to be changed to include terror. It has to be changed from the standpoint of cost because the United States bears far too much of the cost of NATO."

Many of Trump's detractors claimed he wanted to with- draw from NATO entirely. However, political fact-checking proves the Don never said he wanted to withdraw from NATO,

just that he wanted to restructure America's involvement in such - especially with regard to fiscal spending.

In the end, Trump's domestic policy was as polarizing as

the rest of his presidency. He either gained ardent support from his followers or turned off those from the middle and left.

CHAPTER 9

INTERNATIONAL RELATIONS

"North Korean Leader Kim Jong Un just stated that the "Nuclear Button is on his desk at all times." Will someone from his depleted and food starved regime please inform him that I too have a Nuclear Button, but it is a much bigger & more powerful one than his, and my Button works!" ~ Twitter, January 2, 2018

THE COMEBACK KING: DONALD TRUMP'S UNFINISHED BUSINESS

WHEN TRUMP WAS INITIALLY NAMED the Republican nominee for president, there was skepticism on both sides of the aisle due to his often inflammatory rhetoric.

Even members of his own party feared Trump's bombast might not go over well with U.S allies and potentially damage foreign relations. However, there was also a belief that Trump's bombastic tendencies would be subdued once he actually gained the Oval Office.

If history has taught the U.S. anything about Donald Trump, it's that he is not in the habit of toning himself down. If anything, Trump dialed up his rhetoric to eleven and ripped the knob off.

Trump's international relations were just as mercurial as

his other passion projects. In a previous chapter, we discussed his stepping back from the Paris climate agreement. His stance on helping fight climate change did not go over well with other nations. Neither did his changing opinions on the matter of climate change itself.

In 2009, Donald Trump gathered with a number of prom- inent New York businessmen to take out a full-page advertise- ment in *The New York Times*. The statement was

unequivocally adamant that climate change was not only real, but a pressing problem.

"If we fail to act now, it is scientiflcally irrefutable that there will be catastrophic and irreversible consequences for humanity and our planet."

However, fast forward a few years to the Trump presi- dency, and we find that the Don's viewpoint on climate change had radically altered.

Trump's 2020 statement about climate change suggests he takes it seriously, but also doesn't want efforts to fight it to damage the ability of U.S. companies to turn a profit.

"Nothing's a hoax about that. It's a very serious subject... I want the cleanest air, I want the cleanest water. The environ- ment is very important to me. I also want jobs. I don't want to close up our industry because somebody said you have to go with wind."

While President Trump's rhetoric seemed to present a balanced view, critics are quick to point out his actions while holding the Oval Office seem counterproductive to fighting climate change.

The Climate Deregulation Tracker, run by the Sabin Center for Climate Change Law, has documented more than

130 steps the Trump administration has taken to scale back measures to fight climate change. (Cheung, 2020.)

Notable rollbacks on climate protection that were enacted under Trump's watch include the following.

Deciding to withdraw from the Paris climate agreement, which committed the U.S. and 187 other countries to keep rising global temperatures below 2C.

Replacing President Barack Obama's Clean Power Plan, which would have limited carbon emissions from coal and gas- fired power plants, with the Affordable Clean Energy rule, which had weaker regulations.

Attempting to freeze the fuel efficiency standards imposed on new vehicles and prevent California from setting its own emissions rules.

While Trump has never overtly stated that he didn't believe climate change was a problem, his actions as president seem to suggest at least a level of skepticism.

Withdrawing from the Iran Nuclear Deal.

Trump's decision to withdraw from the Iran nuclear deal was covered in a previous chapter. However, it is worth revisiting in the context of Trump's international relations policies.

Trump's withdrawal of the Obama-era deal was in keeping with his anti-globalization stance and his mistrust of foreign powers.

Even after Trump withdrew, Iran continued to hold to the deal, keeping its stockpile of nuclear material under the limits set by the negotiations. However, Trump would make another controversial decision which would cause further friction.

After Trump, in January 2020, ordered a drone strike that killed Iran's top general, Qassem Soleimani, Tehran effectively abandoned the deal altogether. It can be argued that Trump's policies with Iran only increased the likelihood that Tehran would pursue nuclear weapons.

Trade Rows with China, and the "Wuhan Virus."

Trump's hairline stance was in keeping with his America First philosophy and his bombastic approach to international relations.

While his tariffs and the trade wars they incited were controversial, they were at least not inflammatory like some of his other rhetoric. Perhaps the most incendiary of Trump's comments about China came as the COVID pandemic swept the world.

Trump would claim, without providing evidence, that Chinese labs had created the Coronavirus and caused the pandemic. He would later double down on those statements during an interview with Newsmax's Steve Cortes in 2020.

"I had no doubt about it. I was criticized by the press because China has a lot of people taken care of. They took care of Hunter [Biden]. They took care of Joe. They took care of every- body, didn't they? And people didn't want to say China. Usually, they blame it on Russia. It's always Russia, Russia, Russia, but I said right at the beginning it came out of Wuhan."

Trump would argue that the term was appropriate, given that the virus was first identified in Wuhan Lab in China. He also argued that China was not transparent about the early stages of the pandemic and was responsible for the virus's global spread. By using such divisive language, Trump was seen as undermining diplomatic efforts to address the pandemic and promote global cooperation.

CHAPTER 10

DOMESTIC RELATIONS

115

CATHERINE MCCARTHY

"Why are we having all these people from shit-hole coun- tries coming here?"
~White House meeting, January 11, 2018

THE COMEBACK KING: DONALD TRUMP'S UNFINISHED BUSINESS

THE COMEBACK KING has been mired in controversy almost from the moment he came into the world. It should come as no surprise that his domestic relations policies would stir up a great deal of consternation.

The above quote perhaps exemplifies his bombastic, over-the-top mannerisms perfectly. Once again, his words reinforced

to his supporters that he was a man cut from the same cloth as them, while his detractors were driven ever further away.

Other controversial presidents, such as George W. Bush, went out of their way to be seen as uniters, not dividers. Trump threw this conventional wisdom out the window, preferring to double down on his domestic policy stances.

•••

Deregulation of Businesses

In an earlier chapter, we examined how Trump's deregula- tion of banks helped lead to the collapse of the Silicon Valley Bank. But banks were far from the only businesses that Trump deregulated.

Trump argued that the deregulations were necessary to help businesses cut costs and operate more competitively with international rivals. Critics argued that his deregulatory agenda helped the wealthy while hindering lower socio-economic groups.

One of the major areas that Trump targeted for deregula- tion was the oil and natural gas industry. He rolled back regula- tions in the following ways:

Easing Methane Limits

During the Obama administration, regulations were put into place to help combat climate change. One of the chief industries regulated was the natural gas industry. Specifically, the Obama-era regulations limited the amount of methane that a business could produce without penalty.

Trump acted to repeal regulations put in place in 2016 that limit methane emissions from new oil and gas drilling, trans- port, and storage operations. Natural gas is composed mostly of methane, one of the main pollutants scientists link to climate change.

Offshore Drilling

After the fatal Deepwater Horizon drilling disaster of 2010, the Obama administration worked to regulate offshore drilling. Specifically, they

required nonstop monitoring of such sites in an attempt to prevent
another disaster.

However, Trump argued that the regulations were hindering the oil company's profits. His administration hoped that by deregulating offshore drilling they could save oil companies a billion dollars over a ten-year period, which would make U.S.oil production compete on more even ground with foreign sources.

Expansion of Offshore Drilling

The Trump administration ordered a reversal of an Obama-era ban on oil and gas drilling in the Arctic and Atlantic oceans in 2017

Then, the following year, the administration outlined a proposal to open up the Atlantic, Pacific and new parts of the Arctic oceans to offshore drilling. Many of these sights had been previously protected under environmental protection

laws.

Since that plan was announced, six states - including California, New Jersey, Delaware, and New Hampshire - passed legislation or amendments to restrict offshore drilling. The oil and gas industry applauded the president's efforts.

Erik Milito, a vice president of the American Petroleum Institute, said, "We appreciate and support efforts to modernize and improve the governance and efficiency of the permitting and approvals process so that unnecessary barriers to oil and natural gas development are minimized and eliminated."

However, the move would prove controversial, like much of Trump's other policies. With so many court challenges to this

deregulation of the oil and gas industry, it is difficult to tell what effect it will have on Trump's legacy (Phillips-Xia, 2019).

Pipeline Permits

Trump issued executive orders in early 2019 to limit the ability of states to block interstate energy projects, including pipelines, under a provision of the U.S. Clean Water Act. His orders called for a review of rules requiring state certifications for federally approved interstate pipelines and projects.

Trump's energy policies were controversial, but also repre- sent one of his more successful forays into deregulation.

Embracing the Fringe

The past can be studied and understood, and a general consensus can be reached from doing so. Likewise, speculation about the future is crucial when forming long-term plans, particularly with regard to economic and domestic policy. While opinions vary, there are universal understandings involved when studying the past or forecasting the future.

However, no one can truly agree on the present. It's one of humanity's greatest weaknesses. A true-life case of not being able to see the forest for all the trees.

Thus, when we examine President Trump's domestic policy, we must do so viewed through a lens of his intentions. Donald Trump wanted to make America Great Again. The Don himself has admitted to having a certain amount of pride in his accomplishments and has never wanted for ambition. So perhaps he was so desperate to Make America Great Again that he acted on his best intentions and got, at best, mixed results.

Trump's first test came as a protest led by Neo Nazis and involving other white nationalist groups took the news cycle by storm on August

11, 2017. The literal torch-bearing Nazis stormed Charlottesville, Virginia, chanting "White lives matter" and "You will not replace us."

Trump was criticized on several fronts after the Nazi march. Many thought the president should have made some kind of address to the nation following the incident.

Instead, Donald Trump was confronted with the white supremacist rally at a press conference cornering a completely different matter - namely, the executive order he'd signed on infrastructure contracting. The media were eager to hear the Don's thoughts on the rally.

Donald Trump perhaps made a mistake by trying to straddle the same fence Bill Clinton had during his "I didn't inhale" moment in 1992.

Trump was decidedly dodgy in condemning the rally, which added fuel to the fire for those who opposed him. Then he said the following: "You had some very bad people in that group, but you also had people that were very fine people, on both sides."

Technically, Trump did NOT state that he thought Nazis were very fine people at all. He repeatedly insisted he supported only the protestors who were against the removal of a statue of Robert E. Lee. However, in context with his some- what vague position, the quote took on a life of its own.

Enacting New Voting Restrictions

Shortly after Trump lost the election in 2020 to Democratic challenger Joe Biden, he began railing against election rules he felt contributed to his loss.

Trump wanted to curtail early voting and all but eliminate absentee voting.

"There should be a legitimate reason for someone to vote absentee," he said at the Conservative Political Action Confer- ence in Orlando, Florida.

Trump also wanted to stop Sunday voting, citing a "Souls

to the Polls" program run by predominantly black churches in the deep south.

Trump argued the changes were necessary to reduce voter fraud, which he alleged was a huge problem even though there has yet to be evidence to back that position up.

Coming Out Against Affirmative Action

Affirmative Action laws and regulations were intended to deal with the disparity among racial demographics when it comes to education and employment. In a nutshell, the majority of higher education and high-paying jobs were demon- strably held by whites.

Trump took aim at Affirmative Action in an unprecedented way. He went after colleges and Universities that enacted such programs.

In 2018, Trump reversed Obama-era rules that caused Harvard University to consider race in matters of diversifying its campus. Trump indicated that he wanted a "race blind" approach to admissions standards (Green, 2018).

The Trump administration even went so far as to file a lawsuit against Yale University. The lawsuit, as laid out by then-Attorney General Willam Barr, was intended to end discrimination against whites and Asian Americans specifically.

"Yale rejects scores of Asian American and white appli- cants each year based on their race," Barr said in a press conference.

The administration even used the 1964 Civil Rights Act, intended to protect racial minorities, as grounds for suing Yale University.

It's hard to gauge what the legacy of these efforts would have been, as the Biden administration has dropped the Yale lawsuit and failed to appeal a lower court ruling in favor of Harvard's diversity program (Berman, 2021).

The legacy of his domestic policy will continue to be a major issue for the future of American politics and society, with implications for economic growth, social justice, and democ- ratic norms and values.

CHAPTER 11

ABORTION RIGHTS

129

"Women who get abortions should face some form of punishment" ~ MSNBC 2016

THE COMEBACK KING: DONALD TRUMP'S UNFINISHED BUSINESS

THERE IS PERHAPS no issue that more deeply divides the political spectrum than that of abortion.

In this case, abortion refers to a woman terminating the pregnancy of her own volition. For most of the history of the United States of America, abortion rights have been a hodge- podge of rules and regulations which entirely depended upon which state the woman seeking to terminate her pregnancy lived in.

At the time of *Roe v. Wade,* abortion was broadly legal in just four states and allowed under limited circumstances in 16 others.

Jane Roe was a pseudonym for Norma McCorvey, an unmarried, unemployed, and pregnant 22-year-old who had already had two children. When she became pregnant for the third time in 1969, she sought to have an abortion in Texas.

Henry Wade was the district attorney of Dallas County, Texas. It was his job to enforce a state law prohibiting abortions. Thus, Henry Wade was the person McCorvey sued when she sought the abortion.

By the time the case reached the Supreme Court in 1973, McCorvey had already given birth, but her fight for the right to abortion continued past her pregnancy. The conservative- leaning court was thought to be sympathetic to Texas. However, in a landmark 7-2 decision, the court ruled in favor of the plaintiff (Editors, 2018).

The court based its decision on the right to privacy guaranteed by the 14th Amendment to the U.S. Constitution. Since the Constitution trumps state laws, abortion became broadly legal in all 50 states of the union.

During an interview in 1999 on the widely-watched news program *Meet the Press*, Trump would state he was in favor of abortion rights.

"I am very pro-choice," he said simply.

However, by the time of his nomination for president, Trump's views on abortion had evolved and changed. Now he stated he was unequivocally pro-life, though he thought abor- tion should be legal if it protects the woman's life.

During the third presidential debate with Hillary Clinton in 2016, he said the following, illustrating his plans once he took office:

"I am pro-life, and I will be appointing pro-life judges, I would think that that will go back to the individual states. If we put another two or perhaps three justice on, that's really what's going to be. That'll happen automatically, in my opinion, because I am putting pro-life justices on the court. I will say

this: It will go back to the states, and the states will then make a determination." (Impelli, 2020)

The Mexico City Policy

During the 1980s, the rise of Christian Evangelicals as a political force had politicians scrambling to deal with their new clout. Even the president of the United States was not immune to their influence.

In 1984, then-President Ronald Wilson Reagan enacted the Mexico City policy via executive order, in part due to pres- sure from the pro-life movement and Evangelicals. Historically, the policy required foreign non-governmental organizations (NGOs) to certify that they would not "perform or actively promote abortion as a method of family planning" using funds from any source (including non-U.S. funds) as a condition of receiving U.S. government global family planning funding.

President Trump reinstated the policy but also significantly expanded it to encompass the vast majority of U.S. bilateral global health assistance (Mills, 2017).

But what can be enacted by presidential decree can be rescinded by presidential decree. The policy remained in effect through the rest of Reagan's term and the four years George

H.W. Bush served in the Oval Office from 1988-1992.

However, Bill Clinton would rescind the order in 1993 during the first term of his presidency. The policy would remain "off" until the second Bush administration under George W. Bush. It was not until the junior Bush's second term, in 2007 (right before the next presidential election), that the Mexico City Policy would be reinstated, however.

President Obama rescinded the order yet again in 2009, but Trump would reinstate and further expand the Mexico

City Policy during his term. His move was lauded by the pro- life movement and derided by the pro-choice adherents.

As of this writing, the Mexico City Policy has been yet again rescinded by Joe Biden. It remains to be seen if there will be a lasting legacy from Trump's efforts at expansion.

Stacking the Supreme Court Against Abortion Rights

One of Donald Trump's unmitigated success stories has to be his appointment of several arch-conservative judges to the

U.S. Supreme Court. Brett Kavanaugh and Amy Barett were both staunch religious conservatives who made no bones about their opposition to abortion rights.

It would not be until after Trump left office that his plans would come to fruition, however. In 2022, the Supreme Court ruled in a 6-3 decision to overturn *Roe v. Wade*. The matter of abortion rights has now returned to control at the state level. Even if a later iteration of the court reverses the decision or Congress codifies abortion rights into law, Trump will always go down in history as the president who brought down the *Roe*

v. Wade Juggernaut.

Trump's stance on abortion has led to mixed results. The pro-life movement applauded his moves to end abortion, but his critics say he has negatively impacted women's health issues and sent the country backward.

Trump unquestionably kept his campaign promise to pack the court with conservative, pro-life justices and overturn *Roe*

v. Wade. However, whether or not this is a good outcome depends entirely upon who you ask.

Throughout his presidency, he took several actions to restrict abortion access and to support anti-abortion policies, often to the dismay of pro-choice advocates, and they will continue to shape the future of reproductive rights and health in the U.S. for years to come

CHAPTER 12

GAY MARRIAGE AND LGBTQ RIGHTS

"It's like in golf... A lot of people - I don't want this to sound trivial - but a lot of people are switching to these really long putters, very unattractive... it's weird. You see these great players with these really long putters, because they can't sink three-footers anymore. And, I hate it. I am a traditionalist. I have so many fabulous friends who happen to be gay, but I am a traditionalist." ~ New York Times, May 5, 2011

THE ABOVE QUOTE perhaps exemplifies Donald Trump's views on alternative lifestyles. Unlike most of his policy stances, which are bombastic but very clear cut, the Don seemed to try and straddle the fence on the issue of LGBTQ rights.

During the buildup to the 2016 election, Trump declared himself to be an ally of the LGBTQ community. He said this in response to the Orlando nightclub shooting:

"Hillary Clinton can never claim to be a friend of the gay community as long as she continues to support immigration

policies that bring Islamic extremists into our country and who suppress women, gays and anyone else who doesn't share their views or values,"

Trump displayed his political savvy once again, linking his immigration policies to the issue of gay rights (Diamond, 2016).

However, Trump's critics were quick to point out that his running mate, Mike Pence, had a history of acting against LBQGT rights both as a member of Congress and as the governor of Indiana. This seeming dichotomy would not slow the Don down, however.

During a campaign rally in 2016, Trump enthusiastically took a rainbow Pride flag from an audience member and waved it around. This move seemed to signify his support of LGBTQ rights.

The move drew support from Chris Barron, the former GOProud leader. Barron praised Trump as "the most pro- LGBTQ Presidential] candidate ever nominated by either party" on Twitter.

However, Barron seemed ignorant of Trump's promise to "strongly consider" appointing conservative justices to the Supreme Court who would overturn the landmark 2015 deci- sion legalizing gay marriage nationwide.

Trump's seemingly Janus-faced stance on gay rights would be a hallmark of his presidency. In 2019, the Trump adminis- tration refused requests from several U.S Embassy around the world to fly the Pride flag during the month of June, tradition- ally revered as Pride month.

Israel, Germany, and Brazil were among the countries who were denied permission to fly the flag on the official flagpole. However, the administration did not prohibit the embassies from displaying it in other places on embassy grounds.

Trump's record on gay rights is not so cut and dried, however.

He appointed an openly gay man, Richard Grenell, to be his ambassador to Germany. Trump also put Grenell in charge of a campaign to decriminalize homosexuality internationally.

"It is concerning that, in the 21st century, some 70 countries continue to have laws that criminalize LGBTQ status or conduct," according to an official White House statement on the campaign.

The campaign focused more on decriminalizing homosexual relationships and acts rather than expanding gay rights such as the right to marriage (Lederman, 2019)

Trump's campaign came swiftly after the execution of a gay man in Iran earlier that year. Ambassador Grenell had this to say when confronted by members of the media:

"This is not the first time the Iranian regime has put a gay man to death with the usual outrageous claims of prostitution, kidnapping, or even pedophilia. And it sadly won't be the last time. Barbaric public executions are all too common in a country where consensual homosexual relationships are criminalized and punishable by flogging and death."

Trump seemed focused on proving that he really was a friend to the LGBTQ community. However, just a year later, Trump would make another controversial move, this time restricting the rights of transexual people.

In 2020, the Trump administration finalized a regulation for the Health and Human Services Department. In the regulation, protections for transgendered people receiving medical care were rolled back.

When the A$ordable Care Act was passed by the Obama administration, it included a provision where medical personnel and institutions were prohibited from discriminating against people on the basis of their trans status.

Trump's regulation e$ectively nullified these protections,

which led critics to say he was not truly a friend of the T in LGBTQ.

The move was part of a broad Trump administration effort across multiple areas of policy — including education, housing, and employment, as well as health care — to narrow the legal definition of sex discrimination so that it does not include protections for transgender people.

Perhaps the most incendiary thing about the regulation was the date on which it was announced. The regulation came to be on the anniversary of the Orlando gay nightclub massacre and also right in the middle of Pride month. The administration seemed to be sending a message that contradicted Trump's claims to be a "friend" to the community.

In the end, Trump's record on LGBTQ rights is dichoto- mous at best. On the one hand, he waved the pride flag at his campaign rally and sought to end international criminalization of homosexuality. On the other, he rolled back trans rights and touted himself as a traditionalist who thought alternative lifestyles were "weird," likening them to extra-long golf putters.

Some say that Trump's policies may have set back LGBTQ rights by years, if not decades.

As of this writing, though Trump is no longer president, he has made no bones about running for office again in 2024. As part of his campaigning for the nomination of his party, Trump has stated he would sign an executive order directing federal agencies to agencies "to cease all programs that promote the concept of sex and gender transition at any age."

Trump has also vowed to punish healthcare professionals who provide gender-affirming care to minors.

In his pledge, he said if educators or school officials "suggest to a child that they could be trapped in the wrong body," they will be "faced

with severe consequences including potential civil rights violations."
(Assuncao, 2023)

Continuing a recent talking point with right-wing figures like Ron DeSantis, Trump also took aim at the U.S. educational system, which he blames for teaching children to uphold liberal ideas.

Trump has said that if he is reelected, his administration would also push schools to "promote positive education about the nuclear family" and celebrate "rather than [erase] the things that make men and women different and unique."

While Trump's stance on gay rights may be murky, his policies, past and perhaps future, leave no room for ambiguity when it comes to trans rights.

CHAPTER 13

HEALTHCARE

THE COMEBACK KING: DONALD TRUMP'S UNFINISHED BUSINESS

"Nobody knew health care could be so complicated." ~
The Washington Post, 27/2/17

ONE OF THE most divisive issues in the early part of the 21st century in the United States has been the subject of health care.

Health care has long been controversial in America, with seemingly no one being happy with how the industry is run. However, the issue came to a watershed moment in 2010, during Barrack Obama's presidency.

Progressive voices in America had long championed the idea of national healthcare, also called single-payer care. Such programs are already a reality in many other industrialized nations, such as the United Kingdom.

Attempts to get national healthcare in America have often seemed an insurmountable task. In order to address the numerous issues with the current American system, congress passed the Affordable Care Act (ACA) in 2010. Often called

Obamacare as a slang term, the ACA is not a single payer system but rather a series of rules and regulations with the intent to make health care more affordable and protect people with pre-existing conditions from being denied coverage.

The reaction to the ACA has been a mixed bag at best. Progressives don't think it goes far enough, while the conserva- tives believe it's government overreach. Some people have benefited from the ACA, especially those formerly unable to obtain insurance because of their medical conditions.

On the other side, however, are people whose premiums have skyrocketed and those who decry that buying health insurance is mandatory under the law.

Donald Trump, ever the savvy politician, seized upon the ACA as a lightning rod to garner political clout. He stated during his campaign and his presidency that he wanted to repeal and replace the ACA.

During a town hall meeting during the run-up to his presidential candidacy, Trump had this to say about the ACA:

"You have to be hit by a tractor, literally, to use it, because the deductibles are so high, it's virtually useless. It is a disaster. And remember the $5 billion website? $5 billion we spent on a website, and to this day it doesn't work. I have so many websites, I have them all over the place. I hire people, they do a website."

— Town hall meeting, June 16, 2015

However, Trump also made it clear that he would not follow the usual GOP playbook when it came to healthcare - namely, as it pertained to Medicare and Social Security.

"I'm not going to cut Social Security like every other Republican. And I'm not going to cut Medicare or Medicaid." — The Daily Signal, May 21, 2015

In order to deal with what he said were major failings with the ACA, Trump introduced the American Health Care Act

(AHCA.) The legislation was primarily aimed at changing the existing ACA rather than introducing an entirely new system.

Here are some of the provisions for the AHCA:

Elimination of the Individual Mandate - The individual mandate was the cornerstone of the ACA. It required people to maintain at least a minimum level of health insurance or else face a tax penalty from the IRS. The idea was young, healthy people - a demographic which typically does not carry health insurance for a variety of reasons - would be forced to buy plans and, therefore, subsidize the older, sicker Americans.

Replace Subsidies with Tax Credits - Trumpcare aimed to replace Obamacare government subsidies for low- income individuals. Instead, tax credits would be issued for anyone not covered by their employer or through government health insurance.

Allow waivers for essential health benefits - Obamacare required all health insurance policies to provide coverage of "essential benefits" that included maternity care

and mental health, even for beneficiaries who didn't need those benefits. The ACHA proposed to allow for exceptions to this rule.

Remove Protections for Pre-existing Condi- tions - The ACA prevented health insurers from charging higher premiums to people with pre-existing conditions. This was the provision the health insurance industry lobbied the hardest against. The ACHA would have allowed individual states to obtain waivers for private insurance companies to charge people more for pre-existing conditions according to risk pools.

Increase the Rate at Which Older Adults May be Charged for Insurance - insurance premiums for older adults could increase three times to five times the rate of healthy younger adults.

Repeal Medicaid Expansion - The AHCA was set to repeal certain Medicaid expansions and replace them with a fixed amount per beneficiary or a lump-sum block grant for states.

There were fears that the ACHA would have left millions of Americans uninsured had it passed. The legislation initially cleared the House of Representatives in 2017, but a Republican-controlled Senate would ultimately shoot it down.

Trump remained undaunted and continued to pursue ways to eliminate the ACA. Stymied at every turn, even by his own political party, Trump's administration instead found ways to weaken Obamacare overall.

One way Trump went about this was to target the information campaign related to the ACA. The Trump administration sharply reduced support for advertising and exchange naviga- tors while reducing the annual enrollment period to about half the number of days (Thompson, 2020).

The Trump administration also cut ACA subsidies to insurance companies offering coverage on the exchanges. The ACA originally provided subsidies to insurance companies to reduce their risks of losing money if they participated on the exchanges. The Trump administration joined congressional Republicans in reneging on these financial commitments

Trump also took steps to bolster cheaper, less expansive insurance plans. The ACA had strict guidelines for what constituted basic health care. The Trump administration strove to expand access to cheaper coverage that did not meet these quality standards and would siphon off healthier enrollees from the exchanges.

Trump also directed the Department of Homeland Security to foster a rule that authorized officials to treat Medicaid enrollment as a negative factor in reviewing the requests of legal noncitizens to extend their stays or change their status.

Donald Trump made some changes to the American healthcare system. However, he was unable to fully repeal the ACA, and his legacy continues to be a controversial one.

CHAPTER 14 GLOBAL WARMING AND CLIMATE CHANGE

THE COMEBACK KING: DONALD TRUMP'S UNFINISHED BUSINESS

"It's really cold outside, they are calling it a major freeze, weeks ahead of normal. Man, we could use a big fat dose of global warming!" ~ Twitter, October 19, 2015

MANY PEOPLE ASSUME that global warming wasn't thought of until the 1990s, when environmentalism became a popular movement. The truth of the matter is, mentions of global warming and climate change go back much, much further. In fact, the original black and white *Godzilla* film attributes the monster's awakening in part to global warming.

When it comes to climate change, the scientific community is overwhelmingly convinced of two facts.

1. The Earth is getting warmer.
2. Man-made actions are at least in part responsible for the temperature change.

Donald Trump, however, has towed the Republican party

line toward climate change, both as a candidate and as the president of the United States.

As mentioned in a previous chapter, Trump withdrew America's involvement in the Paris Climate Agreement. He has also made some contradictory statements on global warming. While he said he doesn't think climate change is a hoax, he did tweet the following on Twitter:

"The concept of climate change was created for and by the Chinese to make U.S. manufacturing non-competitive." ~ Twitter, 2012.

It's difficult to ascertain what Trump's stance on climate change is, given his seemingly contradictory statements. A clearer picture emerges when one views the actions he took as president.

Besides the aforementioned withdrawal from the Paris Agreement, Trump impacted U.S. environmental policy in a number of ways (Kann, 2021).

Scrapping the Clean Power Plan

During the Barack Obama administration, environmental policy took strides toward being proactive toward global warming.

The Clean Power Plan was one of Obama's signature environmental policies. It required the energy sector to cut carbon emissions by 32 percent by 2030.

However, in October 2017, the Trump administration rolled back the policy via the EPA. Among the reasons cited were unfair burdens on the power sector and a "war on coal" as the president put it.

Dismantling the Once In, Always In policy

Another key environmental protection the Trump administration hindered or dismantled was the Once In, Always In policy (OIAI for short.)

The policy was one of the stiffest measures ever enacted. In 1995, Bill Clinton pushed the policy as part of his overhaul of the EPA.

OIAI said that if a company polluted over the legal limit, it would have to match the lowest levels set by its industry peers. Not only that, but the company would have to match those guidelines indefinitely.

By dropping OIAI, the Trump EPA incentivized compa-

nies to come up with their own solutions to lower pollution, mostly by increasing efficiency. But the controversial aspect was that once the business in question met its goals, it no longer had to abide by them, meaning the solutions could be tempo- rary by their very nature.

Rolling back Obama-era Fuel Efficiency Guidelines

Under the Obama administration's fuel economy targets, cars made after 2012 would have to get 54 miles per gallon by 2025. This move was made in an attempt to curb emissions and fossil fuel usage.

But in August 2018, the Department of Transportation and
the EPA changed the rule. They capped that target number
at 34 miles per gallon by 2021.

The reversal not only had the potential to negatively impact
the environment. It also created legal conflict with certain
states, such as California, who had their own, much higher
emissions caps.

...

Rescinding Obama-era Executive Order on Sea Level Rise.

During the Obama administration, the then-president signed an executive order which required construction projects to factor in rising sea levels if they were partially or wholly funded by the federal government. While some praised the initiative, others said it didn't go far enough since many construction projects were not federally funded at all.

In August 2017, President Trump revoked that executive order with one of his own, ending the requirement. Companies no longer had to factor in sea level rise when engaging in new construction.

In an odd twist, Trump's own Department of Housing and Urban Development would require buildings constructed with disaster relief funds to take sea level rise into account. While not as much a blanket provision as Obama's original executive order, it did put at least some of the protections back in place.

Weakening the Clean Water Act.

Dating all the way back to 1972, the Clean Water Act (CWA) provided protections for what was referred to as U.S. waterways. These included bodies such as Lake Michigan and the Mississippi River.

Revoking or revising the CWA would have been a nigh-insurmountable task for any president. However, Trump's administration found an end around to their dilemma.

In 2017, President Trump issued an executive order directing the EPA to formally review what waters fell under the jurisdiction of the EPA, as well as the Army Corps of Engineers.

Trump's EPA significantly narrowed the definition of what

could be called a protected river or wetland, opening the door to more development and looser protections for the waterways in question.

Making Seismic Air Guns Legal

Seismic air guns is a device utilized by the oil and natural gas industry in oceanic settings. Their purpose is to use tightly focused blasts of sound to refract off the ocean floor in the hopes of detecting hidden deposits of fossil fuels.

Environmental concerns stemmed from fears that the blasts would disorient and potentially kill sonar-using ocean life such as dolphins. There was also debate over whether the seismic blasts could harm plankton, a key link in the ocean food web.

In 2017, the Bureau of Energy Management banned the use of seismic air guns. However, the Trump administration's National Oceanic and Atmospheric Administration (NOAA) reinstated the use of the guns, saying that they did not violate the Marine Mammal Protection Act.

Changing how the Endangered Species Act is Enforced.

In 1973, congress passed the Endangered Species Act. In a nutshell, the act was designed to limit the harm caused by human development on endangered animals and their environments.

After being left largely untouched for over three decades, the Trump administration announced changes to how the act would be implemented.

In July 2018, the Trump administration said more weight would be put on economic considerations when designating an endangered animal's habitat. In other words, if a company's profits could be lessened by protecting an endangered species habitat, then the company would be allowed to begin construc- tion even if it would technically violate the original 1973 law.

Downgrading Climate Change so it is No Longer a National Security Threat.

During the Obama presidency, climate change was declared a national security threat. America was far from the first country to enact such a policy, nor was it the last.

The Trump administration made the decision to delist climate change from national security threats in December 2017.

This meant less Department of Defense research funding and a more nationalistic viewpoint on the potential impacts of wildfires, droughts, hurricanes, and other natural disasters.

Opening Public Lands for Oil and Gas Drilling.

One of the Trump administration's boldest moves was to open up former national monuments to natural gas and oil drilling.

Unlike national parks, which have to be approved by Congress, national monuments can be created by executive order. However, Trump was the first president to claim that the opposite was also true. In other words, the sitting president could dismantle such protections by another executive order.

The Bears Ears national monument and the Grand Staircase-Escalante Park, both in Utah, were reduced vastly in size. They were also opened up for mining and drilling operations.

However, this sweeping executive order has faced rigorous challenges in court, partly from Native American tribes to whom the land originally belonged.

...

Trump and Climate Change Conclusion.

Donald Trump has stated contradictory things about his belief in climate change. His actions as president, however, overwhelmingly reinforce the idea that he puts the economy over the environment.

Trump's attitude to global warming was widely criticized by climate change activists and scientists. Moreover, his denial of the scientific consensus on climate change was seen as contributing to a broader trend of anti-science and anti-intellec- tualism in U.S. politics.

CHAPTER 15

GUN CONTROL

THE COMEBACK KING: DONALD TRUMP'S UNFINISHED BUSINESS

"No matter what you do - guns, no guns - it doesn't matter. You have people that are mentally ill. And they're gonna come through the cracks. And they're going to do things that people will not even believe are possible." ~ Meet the Press, October 4, 2015

ONE OF THE most divisive issues in the United States of America is the concept of gun control.

The current interpretation of the Second Amendment to the Constitution is that all private citizens have the right to bear arms. This has been upheld in numerous court battles, going all the way to the Supreme Court.

However, critics of the nation's gun control policy point out that the amendment properly reads *"the right to bear arms for the purposes of a well-organized state militia."* This would seem to indicate only the state National Guards are constitutionally allowed to bear arms. Critics also point out the vast differences

in technology when the amendment was written. Guns were

single-shot affairs that required a long time to reload, in contrast to today's rapid-fire automatic weapons.

When it comes to gun control, there are varying opinions, but there are certain irrefutable facts as well. Chief among them is the fact that mass shootings have increased dramatically in frequency since 1994 (Boshcema, 2023).

Donald Trump stands out among Republican presidents such as Ronald Reagan and George W. Bush when it comes to gun control. His administration took several steps to curb gun violence after the Stoneman Douglas school shooting in Park- land, Florida. After the tragedy, Trump was quick to give a speech in which even his detractors admitted he sounded presi- dential.

The following excerpt shows a great deal more compassion than one would have expected of the Don, given his bombastic and fiery history of on-the-record statements:

"We must work together to create a culture in our country that embraces the dignity of life, that creates deep and mean- ingful human connections and that turns classmates and colleagues into friends and neighbors."

In the same press conference, he made a statement that had the gun rights movements worried and drew scoffing incredulity from gun control advocates.

"Later this month, I will be meeting with the nation's gover- nors and attorney generals, where making our schools and our children safer will be our top priority. It is not enough to simply

*take actions that makeU.S.feel like we are making a di"erence.
We must actually make that di"erence."*

Gun rights activists worried about what actions Trump was alluding to. The gun control advocates didn't think Trump's actions would amount to much.

...

Fix NICS Act

On March 23, 2018, Trump signed into law the Fix NICS Act.

The act was a bipartisan measure aimed at improving the National Instant Criminal Background Check System (NICS). The act required federal agencies to submit semiannual certifi- cation reports to the attorney general on their compliance with record-keeping and transmission requirements and to come up with plans to increase coordination and automated reporting. It carried financial penalties for political appointees who didn't comply (Robertson, 2019).

Universal Background Checks Support

Donald Trump would hold a bipartisan meeting of Congress to look for solutions to the gun violence problem in America. He expressed support for legislation that would have made universal background checks mandatory for not just gun stores, but private owners who sold their wares at gun shows.

Despite the president's support, the bill failed to pass through the Senate in a narrow vote that, by and large, fell along party lines.

Taking a Stand Against the NRA

The National Rifle Association, or NRA, has one of the most powerful, well-funded lobbying arms in modern politics. They contribute heavily to candidates who support gun rights, often but not always Republicans.

Most GOP politicians don't want to even sound as if they might stand in opposition to the NRA for fear of the potential fallout. The

NRA has a history of funding the opponents of those who speak against gun rights in primaries.

Trump, however, indicated that he would be willing to stand against the NRA in this exchange with Democratic Senator Chris Murphy:

Murphy: And so I think we have a unique opportunity to get comprehensive background checks, and make sure that nobody buys a gun in this country that's a criminal that's seriously mentally ill, that's on the terrorist watch list. But, Mr. President, it's going to have to be you that brings the Republicans to the table on this because, right now, the gun lobby would stop it in its tracks.

Trump: I like that responsibility, Chris. I really do. I think it's time. It's time that a president stepped up, and we haven't had them. And I'm talking Democrat and Republican presidents

— they have not stepped up.

His detractors assumed Trump's tough talk would not be backed up by actual actions. But then soon discovered that they were wrong.

Bump Stock Ban

Bump stocks are devices that can be easily modded onto existing semiautomatic rifles to make them fully automatic. They had been around for years before they entered the U.S. national consciousness.

The devices became part of the national gun debate after a mass shooting tragedy. It was in October 2017 that

64-year-old Stephen Paddock, an avid outdoorsman who was said to have no particular political affiliation, planned and executed one of the most violent mass shootings in U.S. history.

Paddock used AR-style rifles affixed with bump stocks in his assault. His targets were people attending an outdoor country music concert in Las Vegas, Nevada. More than 50 people were killed, and hundreds more were injured.

During the Obama administration, there were several attempts to ban bump stocks. However, the ATF had previ- ously ruled ten times between 2008 and 2017 that certain models could not be prohibited under existing gun laws.

Shortly after the shooting, Trump sent a missive to his Attorney General Jeff Sessions to *"dedicate all available resources to complete the review of the comments received, and, as expeditiously as possible, to propose for notice and comment a*

rule banning all devices that turn legal weapons into machine guns."

The following month, on March 23, the Justice Depart- ment announced it was proposing a rule to that effect. This happened despite vehement objections from the NRA.

The final rule required the owners of any bump stocks to destroy the devices or turn them in at an ATF office before March 26, when the rule went into effect.

Then Trump went one step further. Nine months later, in December 2018, the Department of Alcohol, Tobacco, and Firearms (ATF) announced a blanket bump stock ban.

Rolling Back Gun Control Measures

Donald Trump's moves were not always in opposition to gun control, however. He made frequent campaign promises to protect gun rights, saying they were under attack by the liberal left.

He put that promise into practice on Feb. 28, 2017. Presi- dent Trump signed a bill into law rolling back an Obama-era regulation. The Regulation was intended to make it harder for

people with mental illness to purchase or own guns. That Obama-era measure included people receiving Social Security checks for mental illnesses. It also included a provision to prevent people deemed unfit to handle their own financial affairs to the national background check database.

Arming Teachers and School Staff

In the wake of the Parkland school shooting, Trump would make a controversial suggestion that has since become a right- wing pundit talking point. Namely, he wanted to put guns in the hands of teachers and other school staff. He said the following on February 21, 2018, during a White House "lis- tening session" dedicated to gun violence.

"It's called concealed carry, where a teacher would have a concealed gun on them. They'd go for special training. ... So let's say you had 20 percent of your teaching force, because that's pretty much the number — and you said it — an attack has lasted, on average, about three minutes. It takes five to eight minutes for responders, for the police, to come in. So the attack is over. If you had a teacher with — who was adept at firearms, they could very well end the attack very quickly."

In the end, President Trump's stance on gun control was a mixed bag. While he did ban bump stocks and called for an expansion of the NICS, he failed to implement universal back- ground checks and rolled back some gun control regulations.

CHAPTER 16

TERRORISM

"Donald J. Trump is calling for a total and complete shutdown of Muslims entering the United States Until our country's representatives can figure out what is going on." ~Statement from Trump Campaign staff, December 7, 2015

DONALD TRUMP'S ATTITUDE, policy, and solutions to fight terrorism were a major focus of his presidency, with his administration taking several actions aimed at reducing the threat of terrorism both domestically and internationally.

Executive Order 13769

On January 21, 2017, President Trump would take perhaps the most controversial step of his presidency to combat terrorism. He signed an executive order with multiple facets designed to achieve multiple goals.

However, there was one particular aspect of Executive Order 13769 that drew the ire of his critics - a ban on all travel from seven predominately Muslim countries. Critics called the rule the "Muslim Ban," even though technically, no particular religion is named in the executive order at all.

Commonly referred to as the Trump Travel Ban, the measure was meant to curb terrorism and keep Americans safe. However, critics were quick to point out that the travel ban was at the least prejudiced and at worst bonafide discriminatory and racist.

Although the travel ban from seven majority Muslim countries grabbed the attention, and headlines, of Americans, there were many other facets of the executive order itself (UC Santa Barbara, 2023).

Executive Order 13769 lowered the number of refugees to be admitted into the United States in 2017 to 50,000. Previously the Obama administration had set the number of allow- able refugees into the country at 85,000.

The Executive Order would also suspend U.S. Refugee Admissions Program (USRAP) for 120 days, a period of four months. While the so-called Muslim ban got more attention, this provision had the potential to halt more immigration than any other part of the order.

The countries affected by the travel ban were Iran, Libya, Somalia, Sudan, Syria, and Yemen. Iraq was also included in the original executive order. However, it would be dropped following pointed protests from the Iraqi government. The Trump administration relented on including Iraq only when they received promises of improved vetting of Iraqi citizens in collaboration with the Iraqi government.

In all, the Executive Order led to more than 700 travelers being detained. Also, 60,000 formerly legal visas were provisionally revoked.

President Trump faced the controversy head on, in his

usual idiom. He went on record with Joe Scarborough and used history to create a precedent for his travel ban:

"Take a look at [FDR's] presidential proclamations back a long time ago, 2525, 2526, 2527. What he was doing with Germans, Italians, and Japanese because he had to do it. We have to get a hand around a very serious problem. We're not talking about internment; this is a whole di!erent thing."

The travel ban would be challenged numerous times in court, but provisions of it remained in effect for years until President Joe Biden took office and revoked them in early 2021.

Expanding Drone Strikes and Eliminating Transparency

In the aftermath of the 9/11 terrorist attacks, which notably brought down the World Trade Towers in New York City - Trump's literal backyard - drone strikes became increas- ingly common in the war on terror. A drone strike involves the use of an unmanned, remote-controlled aircraft that either acts

as a guidance system for artillery or is itself an explosive weapon.

Trump would not be the first president to court controversy with drone strikes. President Obama ordered numerous drone

strikes during his presidency against terror targets. International outcry over the alarmingly high civilian death toll in such strikes led President Obama to issue an Executive Order requiring U.S. intelligence officials to publish the number trof civilians killed in drone strikes outside of war zones.

In 2019, President Trump revoked the Obama-era rule with one of his own. Trump cited intelligence reports which stated that the rule revocation was necessary because it would eliminate superfluous reporting requirements, requirements that do not improve government transparency but distract the intelligence professionals from their primary mission of combating terrorism.

The move was met with disdain by the president's critics, particularly those of an international nature, but was met with approval by his base.

President Trump would also greatly expand the use of drones in the war on terror. According to the Bureau of Inves- tigative Journalism, a UK-based think tank, there were 2,243 drone strikes in the first two years of the Trump presidency, compared to 1,878 in Mr. Obama's eight years in office.

The resulting civilian deaths led to greater international

outcry, though it did not deter the Don from continuing to use drone strikes for the remainder of his term in office.

In conclusion, Donald Trump's efforts to fight terrorism

were mired in controversy. Some terrorism experts argued that a more nuanced approach was necessary (Cordesman, 2018), while Trump's supporters pointed to his tough stance on terrorism as a campaign promise kept.

CHAPTER 17

POLITICAL CORRECTNESS

"Things have happened, having to do with many things including political correctness, where people are so worried about being politically correct that they are unable to function." ~ The Economist, September 3, 2015

IT SHOULD COME as no surprise by this point that Donald Trump is not a proponent of the political correctness movement.

Donald Trump's attitude to political correctness was often a divisive aspect of his presidency. He positioned himself as a champion of free speech and as someone who was willing to push back against what he saw as excessive political correctness.

In particular, Trump took to Twitter to sling his politically incorrect brand of political firebrand-ism:

"Lightweight Senator @RandPaul should focus on trying to

get elected in Kentucky-—a great state which is embarrassed by him."-Twitter, 2017.

Trump would lash out at his own political party as well as his traditional detractors. His rhetoric often contained a great deal of insults and hyperbole.

Executive Order Protecting Conservative Voices on College Campuses

In 2019, responding to what he believed was a spate of incidents in which conservative voices and viewpoints were silenced on "liberal" college campuses, Trump signed a new executive order.

Trump announced his planned order at the annual Conservative Political Action Conference (CPAC) in Washington. The event featured activist Hayden Williams, who was punched at the University of California, Berkeley, in February 2018 while recruiting students for a conservative group.

In response to the physical assault of Williams, the Justice Department filed a statement of interest in a free speech lawsuit filed against the university, accusing it of discriminating against speakers with conservative views.

The case was settled when the school agreed to modify its handling of "major events" on campus.

Pushing Back Against Cancel Culture

Donald Trump raised concerns about the phenomenon popularly known as "cancel culture."

He believed that cancel culture, in which people and organizations who do things that displease progressives are attacked with criticism and boycotts, was a factor in stifling free speech. Most especially free speech by conservative voices.

In a speech on the Fourth of July at Mt. Rushmore in 2020, Trump had this to say on cancel culture:

THE COMEBACK KING: DONALD TRUMP'S UNFINISHED BUSINESS

"One of their political weapons is 'cancel culture' — driving people from their jobs, shaming dissenters and demanding total submission from anyone who disagrees. This is the very defini- tion of totalitarianism, and it is completely alien to our culture and our values, and it has absolutely no place in the United States."

This was far from the only time the Don had strong words about the subject. At a speech at the Republican National Convention in 2020, Trump proclaimed that "the goal of cancel culture is to make decent Americans live in fear of being fired, expelled, shamed, humiliated and driven from society as we know it. The far left wants to coerce you into saying what you know to be false, and scare you out of saying what you know to be true."

Trump's fiery, politically incorrect rhetoric led to a marked increase in hate speech online and acts of violence toward marginalized groups (Evans, 2016.)

Trump, however, sought to distance himself from the actions he had incited. He even said in an interview on *60 Minutes* that "I am so saddened to hear that (hate incidents are on the rise). And I say, 'Stop it.' If it—if it helps. I will say this, and I will say right to the cameras: Stop it."

Looking ahead, the legacy of Trump's attitude on political correctness will continue to be a major issue for the future of free speech and open debate in the U.S. His rhetoric and actions were seen by many as contributing to a divisive and polarized political climate, so any future president needs to find the balance between open debate and free expression while also acknowledging the harm that can be caused by hate speech and discriminatory language.

CHAPTER 18

HILLARY CLINTON

193

"If Hillary Clinton can't satisfy her husband what makes her think she can satisfy America?" ~ Twitter, April 16, 2015

THE COMEBACK KING: DONALD TRUMP'S UNFINISHED BUSINESS

IT HAS BEEN SAID that you can judge yourself by the worthiness of your enemies. If that's true, then Donald Trump's numerous criticism and comments on his former rival Hillary Clinton should be viewed in a highly scrutinizing light.

Hillary Clinton served as the first lady of the United States during her husband Bill Clinton's two terms as president. She would go on to be a senator and serve as the secretary of state during Barrack Obama's presidency.

In 2016, Hillary became the Democratic nominee for president. Donald Trump, who had been on friendlier terms with the Clintons in the past, unleashed a storm of incendiary accu- sations and insults at his rival for the office of the presidency.

His tweets during the election campaign linked Clinton to

a National Football League (NFL) controversy starring long- time Patriots Quarterback Tom Brady. Brady had been accused of using improperly inflated balls to gain an unfair advantage.

They had no definitive proof against Tom Brady or #patriots. If Hillary doesn't have to produce Emails, why should Tom? Very unfair!

— Donald J. Trump (@realDonaldTrump) May 11, 2015

Clinton's Emails

Hillary Clinton received a great deal of political backlash for her use of a public email server to transmit sensitive data.

Clinton would even be investigated by the FBI, who ulti- mately cleared her of any wrongdoing. However, Trump was quick to seize upon her emails as a lightning rod for his campaign and presidency, more evidence of his political aplomb.

Clinton's emails would be a frequent subject of Trump's tweets. Here are just a handful of the more than 77 times Trump tweeted about the email scandal of his Democratic rival.

How can Hillary run the economy when she can't even send emails without putting entire nation at risk?— Donald J. Trump (@realDonaldTrump) June 21, 2016

Hillary was involved in the e-mail scandal because she is the only one with judgment so bad that such a thing could have happened!— Donald J. Trump (@realDonaldTrump) July 25, 2016

Look at the way Crooked Hillary is handling the e-mail case and the total mess she is in. She is unfit to be president. Bad judgment!— Donald J. Trump (@realDonaldTrump) November 1, 2016

One of the reasons Hillary hid her emails was so the public wouldn't see how she got rich- selling out America— Donald J. Trump (@realDonaldTrump) June 30, 2016

The new e-mail release is a disaster for Hillary Clinton. At a minimum, how can someone with such bad judgment be our next president?— Donald J. Trump (@realDonaldTrump) January 29, 2016

The invention of email has proven to be a very bad thing for Crooked Hillary in that it has proven her to be both incompetent and a liar!— Donald J. Trump (@realDonaldTrump) July 26, 2016

Crooked Hillary, who embarrassed herself and the country with her e-mail lies, has been a DISASTER on foreign policy. Look what's happening!— Donald J. Trump (@realDonald-Trump) July 16, 2016

We've all wondered how Hillary avoided prosecution for her email scheme. Wikileaks may have found the answer. Obama! — Donald J. Trump (@realDonaldTrump) October 29, 2016

Hillary's sta! thought her email scandal might just blow over. Who would trust these people with national security- Donald J. Trump (@realDonaldTrump) October 16, 2016

Trump would even take aim at his own political appointees on Twitter when it came to the subject of Hillary Clinton's emails.

Attorney General Je! Sessions has taken a VERY weak posi-
tion on Hillary Clinton crimes (where are E-mails & DNC
server) & Intel leakers!— Donald J. Trump (@realDonald-
Trump) July 25, 2017

Trump's Twitter barrage was successful, leading the hashtag #CrookedHillary to trend multiple times.

Donald Trump was accused of using Clinton to distract from some of the controversies of his own presidency. He would often mention Clinton when faced with criticism from the press. His strategy appears to have worked, at least among his base.

In the end, Trump's bitter and hostile attitude toward Clinton would be a hallmark of his presidency, though he did speak less and less of her when Joe Biden was named his chal- lenger for the presidency in 2020.

Trump may have displayed characteristics of a sore winner, but he was able to use Hillary Clinton's lack of charisma and controversial past to make political headway.

CHAPTER 19

DIPLOMACY

201

"Why would Kim Jong-un insult me by calling me 'old,' when I would NEVER call him 'short and fat?' Oh well, I try so hard to be his friend - and maybe someday that will happen!" ~Twitter, November 11, 2017

FORMER PRESIDENT of the United States Teddy Roosevelt once said in terms of diplomacy, it was good to "speak softly and carry a big stick."

To say that Donald Trump eschewed that philosophy during his own presidency is perhaps an understatement.

Donald Trump's presidency was marked by a series of provocative and often inappropriate comments and actions with world leaders. Trump's lack of experience in international diplomacy and his tendency to speak and act impulsively often led to awkward and embarrassing situations with foreign leaders.

...

Kim Jong Un and North Korea

Sometimes called the Hermit Kingdom, North Korea is seen by those outside its borders as a nation ruled by fanatical zealots with absolute authoritarian control. North Korea insists that their philosophy, where the individual disappears in favor of the community dynamic, is morally superior to the rest of the world.

Kim Jong Un was the leader of North Korea during Trump's presidency and remains so as of this writing. Kim Jong Un followed in the footsteps of his father to inherit the role of the supreme leader, an unelected position.

Kim Jong Un and his government have developed a reputa- tion for bombastic statements and antics that are on a par with the Don himself. A favored tactic of the North Koreans is known as "saber rattling," wherein a government threatens or alludes to armed conflict or out-and-out war in order to put pressure on its enemies.

The typical response to North Korean saber rattling has been to minimize or outright ignore it, to avoid giving credence to what most of the world sees as an illegitimate regime. Trump, of course, has never been one to ignore or speak softly about his detractors and enemies.

In response to a speech given by the North Korean foreign minister at the United Nations (UN,) Trump sent the following tweet on September 23, 2017:

"Just heard the Foreign Minister of North Korea speak at the

U.N. If he echoes thoughts of Little Rocket Man, they won't be around much longer."

The Rocket Man nickname references both a song by Elton John and the fact North Korea had recently flubbed the test of a new Intercontinental Ballistic Missile (ICBM), which they claimed could carry a nuclear warhead anywhere in the world.

THE COMEBACK KING: DONALD TRUMP'S UNFINISHED BUSINESS

The phrase "They won't be around much longer" was

strangely not as incendiary as the insulting nickname Trump gave to a foreign leader. This is despite the fact Trump essentially threatened to destroy an entire nation, or at the least kill or depose its leaders.

North Korea, of course, condemned Trump's statement and engaged in even more saber rattling rhetoric than before. But the story does not end there. In fact, the plot twist could not have been created by the most genius-level fiction writer.

Trump and Kim Jong Un became friends. In fact, in an interview with Sean Hannity on Fox News, Trump even went so far as to declare he and Kim had "fallen in love" after his landmark visit to North Korea in 2019.

Donald Trump bucked decades of White House policy and had a summit with the North Korean leader in 2018. The summit was held in Singapore, a tiny nation with good ties with both the U.S. and North Korea.

The summit resulted in no formal agreements between the two nations. However, Trump and Kim would release a joint statement. The following is an excerpt from the most significant passage:

Convinced that the establishment of new U.S.-DPRK relations will contribute to the peace and prosperity of the Korean Peninsula and of the world, and recognizing that mutual con"-dence building can promote the denuclearization of the Korean Peninsula, President Trump and Chairman Kim Jong Un state the following:

1. The United States and the DPRK commit to establish new U.S.-

DPRK relations in accordance with the desire of the peoples of the two countries for peace and prosperity.

2. *The United States and the DPRK will join their efforts to build a lasting and stable peace regime on the Korean Peninsula.*

1 Rea#rming the April 27, 2018 Panmunjom Declaration,

the DPRK commits to work toward complete denuclearization of the Korean Peninsula.

2 The United States and the DPRK commit to recovering POW/MIA remains, including the immediate repatriation of those already identi!ed.

While it was certainly a diplomatic coup, Trump's detrac- tors and many international experts feared that he had granted legitimacy to a dictatorial regime (Pak, 2018).

Then, Donald Trump went a step further. He visited the Hermit Kingdom, meeting with Kim Jong Un personally.

Again, some praised Donald Trump's unprecedented diplomatic overture. But also, again, international experts and Trump's detractors believed he legitimized the dictatorial regime even more.

After the visit, Trump raised further eyebrows - and alarms

- when he expressed both admiration and a desire to be like Kim Jong Un in an impromptu interview with Fox and Friends on the White House Lawn:

"Hey, he's the head of a country, and he's the strong head—he speaks and his people sit up at attention. I want my people to do the same."

For the remainder of Trump's tenure in office, the North Korean dictator would exchange letters with the U.S. presi- dent. Some media wit referred to them as "love letters," and the name stuck, even among Trump's supporters.

The letters provide a fascinating window into their rela- tionship. Kim flatters Trump, writing in flowery prose, and by repeatedly calling him "Your Excellency." Kim wrote in one letter that meeting again would be "reminiscent of a scene from a fantasy film." In another, Kim said that the "deep and special friendship between U.S. will work as a magical force."

Some say that Trump should be praised for opening up the Hermit Kingdom to diplomacy at all, even at the most basic level. Others believe he gave a brutal regime legitimacy. Ultimately history will be the arbiter, but opinions on this remain as bitterly divided as seemingly anything having to do with former president Donald J. Trump.

Queen Elizabeth

There were few monarchs as endearing to the public, both in their home country and abroad, as Queen Elizabeth II.

The queen, before her death in 2022, the Queen was the frequent subject of memes on the internet and a frequent target of pop culture references and puns. The queen always took this status in good stride, even going so far as to knight *Star Trek* actor Patrick Stewart with a fictional Kingon B'athleth rather than the customary sword.

So when Trump made a number of faux pas during a visit to England, people were understandably shocked. Trump shook hands with the monarch, which goes against British protocol. He also walked ahead of the queen while they were doing a ceremonial inspection of the guard, another thing expressly forbidden by royal protocols.

However, what most people remember about Trump's visit to London was the giant, orange diaper-wearing baby blimp flown through the streets of London. Trump felt it was a grave insult and held one person responsible, in particular - London Mayor Sadiq Khan.

Trump said the following in an interview with *The Sun*

newspaper:

"I guess when they put out blimps to make me feel unwel- come, no reason for me to go to London. I used to love London as a city. I haven't been there in a long time. But when they make you feel unwelcome, why would I stay there?"

• • •

Canadian Prime Minister Justin Trudeau

Trump didn't make his feelings about Canada's top elected official ambiguous when he withdrew from the G7 summit in 2018.

PM Justin Trudeau of Canada acted so meek and mild during our @G7 meetings only to give a news conference after I left saying that, "US Tari!s were kind of insulting" and he "will not be pushed around." Very dishonest & weak. Our Tari!s are in response to his of 270% on dairy! — Donald J. Trump (@real- DonaldTrump) June 9, 2018

Trudeau would jab back on social media, stating that Trump only tweeted tough and didn't do so in person. Trump would continue to spar with Trudeau until the end of his term.

French President Emmanuel Macron

The Statue of Liberty was gifted to America by France. For most of their history, the USA and France enjoyed good rela- tions. The good relations took a hit during the second Iraq War, but had largely recovered before Trump took the White House. During a meeting with Macron in 2019, Trump shared an on-camera handshake that was seen as tense at best and a struggle over power dynamics at worst. The handshake would prove prophetic because the two leaders continued to butt heads afterward.

Trump called Macron "Very, very nasty" when the latter criticized the U.S. withdrawing its troops from Syria. Then, Macron would criticize NATO, and Macron upset Trump by calling the 70-year Western alliance "brain dead."

Trump said in response during a press conference shortly after the meeting: *"Nato serves a great purpose. I think that's very insulting. Nobody needs Nato more than France. It's a very dangerous statement for them to make."*

The Don also engaged in a bit of locker room talk with Macron's wife, telling her she had a "great body" and that she was "beautiful." Many in France and the USA found the comments insulting or even constituting sexual harassment.

Vladimir Putin

There is one world leader Trump got along exceptionally well with besides Kim Jong Un. That personage is Russian President Vladimir Putin.

Putin was long criticized by the West and even his own people for human rights abuses and for running a brutal regime rife with assassinations and secret prisons. Trump not only eschewed talking about any such abuses of power, but he also went so far as to praise the way Putin ran his country.

"The man has very strong control over a country. Now, it's a very di"erent system and I don't happen to like the system, but certainly in that system, he's been a leader. Far more than our president has been a leader." (national security forum, September 7, 2016)

Donald Trump's business interests in Russia were seen by some as a potential conflict of interest. But the Don refused to give credence to those accusations, instead emphasizing what a good relationship he enjoyed with Vladimir Putin.

Chinese President Xi Jinping

Communist China has faced international backlash for its authoritarian regime and human rights abuses almost since its inception. President Nixon was the first U.S.leader to open relations with China following the communist revolution, but relations between the two countries have remained tense.

Trump's trade war with China certainly fanned the flames

of discontent behind the Bamboo Curtain. However, when Trump personally met with Xi Jinping, he seemed to express not just respect for Xi, but open admiration.

"And I like President Xi a lot. I consider him a friend, and – but I like him a lot. I've gotten to know him very well. He's a strong gentleman, right? Anybody that – he's a strong guy, tough guy." (G20 Summit June 30, 2019)

"President Xi, who is a strong man, I call him King, he said, 'But I am not King, I am president.' I said, 'No, you're president for life and therefore, you're King.' He said, 'Huh. Huh.' He liked that." (Press conference at the White House, April 2, 2019)

Trump was criticized for being too deferential with Xi and ignoring his poor human rights track record.

Turkish President Recep Tayyip Erdogan

Erdogan, a far-right fundamentalist politician, has been criticized for a brutal regime that cracks down on women's rights and seeks to stifle criticism of the government.

However, Trump would once again ignore the bad in order to praise what he saw as the good, drawing criticism from the

U.S. and abroad, though, as usual, his supporters would only grow stauncher in their belief Trump had done the right thing.

Trump said this about Edrogan.

"President Erdogan. He's tough, but I get along with him. And maybe that's a bad thing, but I think it's a really good thing." (Press conference in Osaka, Japan, June 29, 2019)

THE COMEBACK KING: DONALD TRUMP'S UNFINISHED BUSINESS

"Well, thank you very much. It's my honor to be with a friend of mine, somebody I've become very close to, in many respects, and

he's doing a very good job: the President of Turkey." (Joint press conference with Edrogan, June 29, 2019)

Overall, Trump's comments about world leaders were seen by many as inappropriate and unbecoming of a U.S. president. His rhetoric and behavior often undermined the norms of international diplomacy and contributed to a sense of confu- sion and uncertainty about U.S. foreign policy. His faux pas were seen by many as a reflection of his lack of experience in international diplomacy.

CHAPTER 20

217

COVID

THE COMEBACK KING: DONALD TRUMP'S UNFINISHED BUSINESS

"We have it totally under control. It's one person coming in from China. It's going to be just flne." ~Twit- ter,01/22/2020

WHEN DONALD TRUMP took office in 2016, his supporters and detractors knew he had many challenges ahead. What few were able to predict, other than epidemiologists, was the surge of a new pandemic that would sweep to all four corners of the world.

When the virus began to emerge on the world stage, Trump initially took a stance to downplay its significance, as the tweet that opened this chapter illustrates very well.

Donald Trump would continue this policy of downplaying the pandemic for months. At the end of February, he tweeted the following.

"The Coronavirus is very much under control in the USA...

the Stock Market starting to look very good to me!" February 24, 2020.

But the virus continued to spread. In March, the World Health Organization (WHO) categorized the coronavirus as a pandemic due to its alarming spread and severity.

Trump would refuse to institute a national lockdown, as many other industrialized nations had done. He said that "the cure can not be worse than the disease," referring to the economic drawbacks of locking down all but the most essential workers to quarantine in their homes.

Donald Trump would go on to sign several relief bills, the third of which was passed in March. But these measures did not slow the virus much, and the day after WHO declared the pandemic, the U.S. became the country with the highest confirmed cases of COVID (Lewis, 2021).

The U.S. would continue to hold the ignoble distinction until the end of Trump's presidency.

Trump's early response to the pandemic was criticized by many public health experts and politicians, who argued that he was not taking the crisis seriously enough. Some argued that his initial response to the pandemic contributed to a delay in the implementation of policies and resources that could have saved lives.

The Don would then say something that made him the subject of late-night talk show monologue fodder as well as thousands of memes. In April 2020, upon hearing that bleach could be used to destroy the virus on surfaces, he gave some impromptu medical advice.

"And then I see the disinfectant where it knocks it out in a minute. One minute. And is there a way we can do something like that, by injection inside or almost a cleaning?"

Medical officials were quick to point out that injecting

bleach was not only ineffective as a treatment for the virus but also potentially harmful to anyone who attempted it.

Trump did finally start taking the virus more seriously. He imposed travel restrictions on people coming from China in the first months of the pandemic.

Faced with a rising death toll and a shortage of Personal Protective Gear, the U.S. finally entered a lockdown on nonessential businesses. The lockdowns were necessary, according to disease experts, in order to flatten the curve and reduce the strain on overcrowded hospitals and exhausted healthcare workers.

Trump had predicted the economic consequences would be severe, and he was proven right. The year of 2020 was the worst period for economic growth in the U.S. in almost sixty years (Lewis, 2019).

In order to deal with the economic fallout, Trump signed approval for stimulus checks to help the economy recover. The administration also helped foster legislation that put a morato- rium on evictions and extended unemployment benefits past their normal deadlines.

When WHO criticized the U.S. pandemic response, Trump famously chose to withdraw the country from the orga- nization entirely.

In conclusion, the Trump administration's response to the pandemic was all the more controversial for its seeming ineffec- tiveness. Donald Trump repeatedly said his response to the pandemic was excellent, saying, *"I couldn't have done it any better."*

Trump would also claim the media blew the pandemic out of proportion in an attempt to cost him votes in the 2020 election.

"We have made tremendous progress with the China Virus, but the Fake News refuses to talk about it this close to the Elec-

tion. COVID, COVID, COVID is being used by them, in total coordination, in order to change our great early election numbers. Should be an election law violation!." October 25, 2020, Twitter.

As of this writing, the pandemic may not be entirely over, but most of the restrictions caused by its most acute phase have been lessened, if not eliminated. Only history will truly be able to judge the Trump administration's pandemic response in an objective light.

CHAPTER 21

SOCIAL MEDIA AND TWITTER

THE COMEBACK KING: DONALD TRUMP'S UNFINISHED BUSINESS

*"Social media, where I'm head and shoulders above everybody else. I've read now 22 million people on Twit- ter, Facebook and Instagram. More than 22 million people. Nobody else is even close." ~*Twitter, August 10, 2016

DONALD TRUMP'S relationship with social media was one of the defining features of his presidency. One of the most notable aspects of Trump's social media presence was his use of Twit- ter. He used the platform to share his thoughts on a range of topics, from policy issues to personal attacks on his opponents. His tweets often received widespread attention in the media, with some arguing that they were a way for him to bypass the traditional news media and communicate directly with his supporters.

While Trump's use of Twitter was praised by some for its directness and effectiveness, it was also criticized for being divi- sive and damaging to democratic norms (Kamarck, 2021).

His tweets were often seen as spreading misinformation and conspiracy theories.

"All of the recent Biden claimed States will be legally challenged by U.S. for Voter Fraud and State Election Fraud. Plenty of proof – just check out the Media. WE WILL WIN! America First!"— Donald J. Trump (@realDonaldTrump) November 5, 2020

After George Floyd was murdered by police officers in Minneapolis, Minnesota, protests erupted in response. Trump's tweets were accused of fanning the flames of violence, and inspired vigilante actions like those taken by Kyle Rittenhouse.

....These THUGS are dishonoring the memory of George Floyd, and I won't let that happen. Just spoke to Governor Tim Walz and told him that the Military is with him all the way. Any di"culty and we will assume control but, when the looting starts, the shooting starts. Thank you!— Donald J. Trump (@re- alDonaldTrump) May 29, 2020

However, despite seemingly violating Twitter's policies on inciting violence and misinformation, Trump's account was never suspended, though some of his tweets were flagged.

That is, until he left office. Shortly following the attempted insurrection by Trump supporters on January 6 at the Capitol (which will be covered in the next chapter), Twitter made the decision to permanently ban the Don's Twitter account.

The tweets violated the company's policy against the glorification of violence, Twitter said, and *"these two Tweets must be read in the context of broader events in the country and the ways in which the President's statements can be mobilized by different audiences, including to incite violence, as well as in the context of the pattern of behavior from this account in recent weeks."*

In typical fashion, Trump did not take the news lying down.

Trump sought to test Twitter's ban evasion policy at roughly 8:30 p.m. ET Friday evening on January 8, when he or someone acting on his behalf published four tweets from the @POTUS account.

"As I have been saying for a long time, Twitter has gone further and further in banning free speech, and tonight, Twitter employees have coordinated with the Democrats and the Radical Left in removing my account from their platform, to silence me," Trump tweeted.

The tweets were taken down almost immediately, though the POTUS account remained active.

In response to his social media bans, Trump created his own social media service, Truth Social. The service has flour- ished under his influence, though critics say Truth Social has become a safe haven for white supremacists and oppressive voices.

CHAPTER 22

THE CAPITOL RIOTS

"All of U.S. here today do not want to see our election victory stolen by emboldened radical-left Democrats, which is what they're doing. And stolen by the fake news media. That's what they've done and what they're doing. We will never give up, we will never concede." ~Speech to the Capitol shortly before the riots, January 6, 2021

ONCE THE VOTES were tallied in the November 2020 presidential election, Joe Biden emerged as the clear winner in both the popular vote and the electoral college.

Trump began casting doubt on the legitimacy of the election before it even concluded when early projections had Biden winning by a wide margin.

STOP THE COUNT!— Donald J. Trump (@realDonald-Trump) November 5, 2020

After the election ended, Trump would continue to dial up his attempts to discredit the 2020 presidential election. His tweets and statements about widespread voter fraud leading to his defeat were echoed on right-wing media outlets like Fox News and One America Network.

Trump's lawyers, like Sidney Powell, would also file dozens of lawsuits alleging voter fraud in an attempt to stop the 2020 election from being certified.

Trump also suggested that Mike Pence, as vice president, had the authority to discount "fraudulent" votes, even though the VP's role in certifying election results has traditionally been viewed as ceremonial only.

If Vice President @Mike_Pence comes through for us, we will win the Presidency. Many States want to decertify the mistake they made in certifying incorrect & even fraudulent numbers in a process NOT approved by their State Legislatures (which it must be). Mike can send it back!—January 6, 2021, Twitter.

Trump's speech at the Capitol was said to have fired up the crowd of his angry supporters. They began a riot, which turned into something that hadn't occurred since the War of 1812 - the

U.S. Capitol was invaded.

The mob of Trump supporters broke into the capitol build- ing, prompting an unprecedented evacuation and halting - albeit temporarily - the certification of the 2020 election results. People around the world looked on in shock as Trump supporters attacked members of law enforcement, damaged the capitol building itself, and chanted slogans about "stop the steal" and "hang Mike Pence."

Whether or not the Capitol riots can be characterized as full-scale insurrection hasn't been entirely decided by history yet. However, it is clear that the president's fiery rhetoric directly contributed to the mob's actions.

For his part, Trump would eventually go on Twitter and attempt to calm down his supporters.

Please support our Capitol Police and Law Enforcement.

They are truly on the side of our Country. Stay peaceful!—January 6, 2021, Twitter.

I am asking for everyone at the U.S. Capitol to remain peaceful. No violence! Remember, WE are the Party of Law & Order – respect the Law and our great men and women in Blue. Thank you!—January 6, 2021

He would also tell his supporters to disperse in another tweet, though he also used the opportunity to fan the flames of election denial.

*These are the things and events that happen when a sacred landslide election victory is so unceremoniously & viciously stripped away from great patriots who have been badly & unfairly treated for so long. Go home with love & in peace. Remember this day forever!-*January 6, 2021.

Donald Trump continues to deal with the fallout from the January 6 riots, including a congressional investigation in which his own vice president appears poised to testify against him. The outcome of the investigation remains unclear, but the events of that day will likely be remembered as a turning point in American politics, marking a new level of polarization and division that will continue to shape the country for years to come.

CHAPTER 23

THE 2024 PRESIDENTIAL CAMPAIGN AND INDICTMENTS

"In order to make America great and glorious again, I am tonight announcing my candidacy for president of the United States." ~*Truth Social,* November 15, 2022

EVER SINCE HE lost the 2020 election, which he continues to claim was stolen, Trump has been clear in his intentions to run for office again.

Polls have consistently shown him to have a numerical advantage over rivals like Governors Ron DeSantis (FL) and Greg Abbott (TX) with Republican voters. However, the GOP has seemed reluctant to confirm if he will be their nominee in 2024.

Further complicating the Don's future presidential bid is his recent (as of this writing) indictment in New York on 34 felony counts relating to hush money he allegedly paid to former adult film star Stormy Daniels in the lead-up to the 2016 election.

Trump has been arrested, arraigned, and released on his own recognizance as of this writing. He has chosen to plead not guilty to the charges but remains the only former president to be indicted for a crime in U.S. history.

Trump has vowed to prove his innocence, and in typical fashion, has used social media to lash out against District Attorney Alvin Bragg, who filed the indictment, and the judge assigned to his case, Juan Merchan. He called Bragg a "Soros backed Animal" and posted a picture of a baseball bat next to the DA's head on Truth Social.

He also suggested that the DA should prosecute himself.

"Wow! District Attorney Bragg just illegally LEAKED the various points, and complete information, on the pathetic Indict- ment against me. I know the reporter and so, unfortunately, does he. This means that he MUST BE IMMEDIATELY INDICTED."

"Now, if he wants to really clean up his reputation, he will do the honorable thing and, as District Attorney, INDICT HIMSELF." —April 3, 2023, Truth Social.

On the same platform, he said the following about Judge Merchan...after the judge warned Trump about making incen- diary posts that might incite violence or unrest.

"ADDITIONALLY, THE HIGHLY PARTISAN JUDGE & HIS FAMILY ARE WELL KNOWN TRUMP HATERS. HE WAS AN UNFAIR DISASTER ON A PREVIOUS TRUMP RELATED CASE, WOULDN'T RECUSE, GAVE HORRIBLE JURY INSTRUCTIONS, & IMPOSSIBLE TO DEAL WITH DURING THE WITCH HUNT TRIAL. HIS DAUGHTER WORKED

FOR "KAMALA" & NOW THE BIDEN-HARRIS CAMPAIGN. KANGAROO COURT!!!"

Perhaps seeking to score political points with the staunchest of the Republican voter base, several GOP House members sought testimony from DA Alvin Bragg. House Judi- ciary Committee Chairman Jim Jordan, Oversight Committee Chairman James Comer, and Administration Committee

THE COMEBACK KING: DONALD TRUMP'S UNFINISHED BUSINESS

Chairman Bryan Steil were the most vocal. They claimed that they wanted to investigate alleged improprieties in how Bragg was handling the Trump indictment.

However, congress had no legal authority to compel Alvin Bragg to testify. When Bragg declined to appear before Congress and give testimony, they turned to legislation in an attempt to protect Donald Trump from the legal repercussions of his cover-up of the Stormy Daniels affair.

In a letter sent to Bragg's office on March 25, 2023, the republican controlled house laid out a plan to restructure parts of the Federal Election Campaign Act. While the language leaves the exact method and implementation of these changes rather vague, it implies that the ability to prosecute presidential candidates might be stripped from local and state authorities.

"In light of this fact, to bring uniformity to the law and prevent future attempts by state or local prosecutors to pursue politically motivated prosecutions related to campaign finance regulations applicable to federal elections, Congress may elect to consider legislation that broadens the preemption provision in the Federal Election Campaign Act. This reform could have the effect of better delineating the prosecutorial authorities of federal and local officials in this area and blocking the selective or politicized enforcement by state and local prosecutors of campaign finance restrictions pertaining to federal elections." - Congressional Letter to DA Alvin Bragg's office, March 25th, 2023.

The letter also laid out a plan to curtail the powers of special counsels in future investigations.

"Because the circumstances of this matter stem, in part, from Special Counsel Mueller's investigation,17 Congress may consider legislative reforms to the authorities of special counsels and better delineate their relationships with other prosecuting entities".

Again, there were no specific details included as to what nature these "reforms" would take, but the implied threat was to strip the states of their power to prosecute highly visible indi- viduals like Donald Trump.

Perhaps the most bold move of all made by the GOP-controlled Congress was to propose changes to criteria for federal funding of local law enforcement and justice depart- ments. Congress sought to add in a caveat for "Public Safety" because, in their words, Alvin Bragg's policies have caused crime to skyrocket in New York.

"The Committee on the Judiciary certainly may consider legislation to tie federal funds to improved public safety metrics."

However, the GOP was faced with criticism after legal experts weighed in. The experts concurred that laying the blame or credit at any one individual's feet was, at best narrow- minded and, at worst, cherry-picking.

"We have a tendency to want to blame one person, or credit one person, when in reality these are complex systems that rise and fall for often complex, random reasons that we don't have the ability to explain – but it's easier to say, 'It was Joe Schmoe over there,'" -Jeff Asher, crime analyst t and co- founder of the firm AH Datalytics in a CNN interview, March 18, 2023.

The House GOP's claims were met with hard-line fact-checking by the media, who pointed out that crime in New York City, in particular violent crime, has in fact been on a steady decline for decades. (Dale, 2023)

However, the case against Trump is not necessarily a slam
dunk. While there seems to be little doubt that Trump used
campaign funds to pay hush money to porn actress Stormy
Daniels and another woman rumored to be a former
playmate, the fact remains no one is certain whether or not
Trump can

actually be successfully prosecuted for such under New York's laws.

In particular, it seems that New York's law requires that DA Bragg prove that Trump not only falsified records (which it seems almost certain that he did) Bragg must also prove that Trump did so *in order to cover up a crime*. That's the caveat

that must be dealt with in order for the charges to stick and for Trump to be convicted. However, no case in New York has yet set a legal precedent for a situation like the one Trump finds himself in. (Millhiser, 2023)

In essence, by spending campaign funds to silence his former mistresses, Trump may have violated the federal law... but he has not, in fact, violated New York State law. These murky legal waters may be impossible for Bragg to successfully navigate his way through to a conviction of the former president.

The Rule of Lenity

Way back in 1892, the Supreme Court of the United States first invoked the Rule of Lenity. Fearing that too many local prosecutions were enabling a "march to the gallows" for defendants, particularly those of color, SCOTUS sought to invoke more lenity in the prosecution of offenses.

"Fair warning should be given to the world, in language that

the common world will understand, of what the law intends to do if a certain line is passed."

It could be argued in the court that Donald Trump and his campaign did not know they were violating the law because it was not spelled out clearly enough what violating the law meant. The Rule of Lenity has been used to challenge everything from federal fishing mandates to local speed limits, many

times successfully. Whether or not Trump's team can use the

Rule of Lenity to keep him from being convicted remains to be seen.

In a final twist, the statute of limitations could come into effect. Trump's alleged crimes occurred more than five years ago, past the normal limit for a felony. If the charges are somehow reduced to misdemeanors, then Bragg's office has an even harder sell. Misdemeanor statutes expire at two years.

Jean E. Carroll

Longtime, magazine writer and part-time novelist Jean E. Carroll, is certainly no stranger to controversy. Her unflinching feminism has weathered the storm of conservative attacks for decades, but she was thrust into a whole new spotlight upon the publication of her memoir "What Do We Need Men For? A Modest Proposal" in 2019.

Her feminist autobiography alludes to a Jonathon Swift (of *Gulliver's Travels* fame) tongue-in-cheek proposal, in which he suggested that eating children would be a good way to deal with hunger and overpopulation. Jean E. Carroll's memoir likewise proposes in a tongue-in-cheek way that men should be done away with entirely, leaving behind a females-only planet.

The book covers her entire life and long career and has been described as "exhaustive" by critics. However, it's one relatively small section that has garnered a ton of attention... and led to Trump losing a civil defamation case in court.

In her book, Jean E. Carroll alleges that Trump raped her in a department store in 1996. Her stunning accusation came amid the #MeToo movement, which thrust the abuse and assault of women into a new spotlight.

Perhaps predictably, Carroll's allegations were harshly scrutinized in both traditional and social media. Many asked the question of why she had not come forward earlier. Carroll said that there were several reasons why she did not.

Carroll testified in court that she feared repercussions on her career from Trump's formidable legal team. She also cited the culture of the 1990s, which was often not sympathetic to rape victims and put them on trial in the court of public opinion.

Perhaps most troubling of all, Carroll also alleged fears that her accusations would only make Trump even more popular among his followers.

Trump was quick to denounce and deny Carroll's allega- tions. He claimed she was making the accusation of rape in order to sell her "really crummy book" and that she "wasn't his type."

Trump's words would have ramifications he did not consider. Trump possibly believed that since the statute of limi- tations had expired on the rape charges, that he was out of any legal danger. However, a change to New York state laws would enable Jean E. Carroll to seek justice another way.

In 2022, New York's legislature successfully passed the Adult Survivors Act. In the act's provisions, adult survivors of a previous assault had a one year window in which to file a civil claim against their abusers.

Jean E. Carroll filed a civil suit against Trump for the rape and also for libel, alleging he had damaged her reputation and career.

Carroll's testimony was presented to the jury. When asked why she had filed the suit, Carroll had this to say:

"I'm here because Donald Trump raped me, and when I wrote about it, he said it didn't happen. He lied and shattered my reputation. I'm here to try and get my life back."

Trump's team faced a difficult uphill battle because of the difference between criminal and civil cases. In a criminal case, the prosecution must prove that the defendant is guilty beyond a reasonable doubt.

However, in a civil case, the jury is tasked with considering the "preponderance of evidence." While the preponderance of evidence is a broad legal term with many ramifications and facets, the way in which it applied to the Trump case used the former president's own words and actions against him.

Carroll's lawyers argued, successfully that the preponderance of evidence in this case meant that the accusations against Trump were more likely to be true than false. The judge reminded the jury to put the concept of reasonable doubt out of their minds and proceed under the preponderance of evidence instead.

Because of the former president's claims of being able to "grab 'em by the P***y," Carroll's lawyers had formidable ammunition in the case. They were also able to bring up tons of online harassment Carroll endured after her allegations against the former president were made public, proving Trump had damaged her reputation and ability to earn a living.

In the end, the jury did not find that Carroll had presented enough evidence to prove she'd been raped. However, they concluded that Trump had "sexually abused" her, a slightly lower charge.

They also found the former president guilty of libel in his defamation of Carroll in social media.

Despite claiming he was going to confront his accuser, Trump never testified in the case. He did, however, give a videotaped deposition which was played for the court. In the deposition, Trump reiterated his earlier talking points. He said that Carroll was lying about the assault, that she wasn't even his type, and that she was just trying to hamstring him politically as well as financially.

In the end, the Jury sided with Carroll. They awarded the

magazine writer with $2 million in damages for the sexual abuse and $3 million in damages for libel and defamation.

As of this writing, Trump's legal team has filed an appeal against the decision. However, his legal troubles with Jean E. Carroll seem to be just beginning, not ending. In May 2023, she filed a new defamation lawsuit over the social media rants Trump produced following the verdict. This new lawsuit seeks no less than $10 million in damages due to his defamation, potentially harming her reputation and ability to earn a living.

Even with Trump's loss in court, where a jury found him liable of sexual abuse and libel, he remains, as of this writing, the GOP frontrunner for the 2024 presidential election. According to a poll by nonpartisan entity FiveThirtyEight, Trump continues to hold a staunch lead over his closest rival, Florida Governor Ron DeSantis.

In fact, Trump leads DeSantis by more than 20 percentage points, an almost insurmountable lead. The president's polling numbers have steadily increased among GOP registered voters in the period from March to May 2023. (FiveThirtyEight, 2023.)

It would appear that Jean E. Carroll's dark prediction came true. Donald Trump's support among his followers only increased following his loss in court and his indictment by DA Alvin Bragg.

If Trump manages to secure the nomination in 2024 and then wins the presidential election that follows, then he might be immune to further prosecution...and he might not. With the unpredictable nature of the political climate, and possible changes by Congress to protect the former president, it remains to be seen if Trump will ultimately triumph over his numerous political enemies, both in the criminal and civil arenas.

As of this writing, it's unclear what Trump's legal future

looks like or whether he will defeat the charges (and potential charges) arrayed against him.

But Donald Trump isn't called the *Comeback King* for nothing. One pattern emerges quite clearly from the research done for this tome – every time that it seems as if Trump has finally done or said or tweeted something to end his political career, he rises from the ashes like the proverbial Phoenix. He still continues to poll well when compared to other potential Republican 2024 presidential candidates, and his influence and reach appear just as strong as ever.

Only time will tell if Donald Trump will once again sit in the Oval Office. One thing is for certain - it would be a mistake to count him out.

REFERENCES

AlJazeera. 2020 "How Donald Trump's COVID-19 illness unfolded: A timeline."

Aljazeera, October 7, 2020

Alvarez, Priscilla. 2020 "Supreme Court to hear challenges to Trump border wall funding and asylum policies" CNN Politics, October 19 2020.

Assuncao, Muri. 2023. "Trump outlines plan to attack trans rights if re-elected, vows to 'protect children from left-wing gender insanity." New York Daily News, February 1, 2023.

Berenson, Tess. 2018. "President Trump Pulls U.S. Out of 'Defective' Iran Nuclear Deal." Time Magazine, Mayf 18, 2018.

Berman, Dan. 2021. "US drops discrimination lawsuit against Yale." CNN Politics, February 3, 2021.

Bliss, Laura. 2020 "How Trump's $1 Trillion Infrastructure Pledge Added Up." Bloomberg, November 11, 2020.

Boschema, Janie. 2023. "Mass Shootings in the US Fast Facts." CNN, January 24, 2023

Cheung, Hellier. 2020. "What does Trump actually believe on climate change?" BBC News, January 23, 2020.

Cordesman, Anthony H. 2018. "Terrorism: U.S. Strategy and the Trends in Its "Wars" on Terrorism." Center for International Studies Special Report. August 18, 2018.

Dale, Daniel. 2023. "Fact check: Here's the truth about crime in Manhattan." CNN Politics, April 17, 2023.

Diamond, Anna. 2018 "The Original Meanings of the "American Dream" and "America First" Were Starkly Different From How We Use Them Today" Smithsonian Magazine, October 2018.

Diamond, Jeremy. 2016. "Donald Trump to LGBT community: I'm a 'real friend.'" CNN, June 13, 2016.

Editors, History.com. 2018. "Roe v. Wade." History, March 27, 2018.

Evans, Carter. 2016. "Hate, Harassment Incidents Spike since Trump Election." CBS World News, November 16, 2016.

Green, Erica. 2018. "Trump Officials Reverse Obama's Policy on Affirmative Action in Schools." The New York Times, July 3, 2018.

Hansen, Claire. 2022 "How Much of Trump's Border Wall Was Built?" Us News and World Reports, February 7, 2022.

Hamlin, Abby. 2017 "What does Trump's 'Buy American, Hire American' order actually do?" The San Diego Union-Tribune, April 17, 2027

Hutzler, Alexandra. 2023. "What to know about the Trump-era rollback of bank rules and Silicon Valley Bank's demise." ABC News, March 15, 2023.

Impeli, Matthew. 2020. "Donald Trump's Views on Abortion and Roe v. Wade in His Own Words."

Newsweek, September 29, 2020.

Jacobson, Louis. 2020. "Vast majority of workers still don't have paid leave, though federal workers do." Politifact, July 15, 2020.

Kann, Drew. 2021. "'The lost years': Climate damage that occurred on Trump's watch will endure long after he is gone." CNN, January 18, 2021.

Karmack, Elaine. 2021. "Did Trump Damage American Democracy?" Brook- ings Institute, July 13, 2021.

Lewis, Tanya. 2021. "How the U.S. Pandemic Response Went Wrong—and What Went Right—during a Year of COVID." Scientific American, March 12, 2021

Lederman, Josh. "Trump administration launches global effort to end criminal- ization of homosexuality." NBC News, February 19, 2019.

Margolin, Emma. 2016 "'Make America Great Again'—Who Said It First?" NBC News, September 9, 2019

McGrath, Matt. 2020. "Climate change: US formally withdraws from Paris agreement." BBC News, November 4, 2020.

McGraw, Meredith. 2017 "A timeline of Trump's immigration executive order and legal challenges." ABC News, February 29, 2017

Mills, Curt. 2017. "Trump Reinstates International Abortion Funding Ban." US News and World Reports, January 23, 2017.

Millhiser, Ian. 2023. "The Dubious Legal Theory at the Heart of Trump's Indictment." Vox, April 4, 2023.

Owen, Quinn. 2019 "Revamped DACA protections and stripped safeguards: Details of Trump's border wall 'compromise'" ABC News, January 23, 2019

Pak, Jung H. 2018. "Around the halls: Brookings experts react to the Trump- Kim Jong-un summit in Singapore." Brookings Institute, June 12, 2018

Palmer, Doug. 2021. "America's trade gap soared under Trump, final figures show." Politico, February 5, 2021

Phillips, Anna, and Xia, Rosanna 2019. "Trump might limit states' say in offshore drilling plan. Here's how." The Los Angeles Times, May 21, 2019. Popken, Ben. 2017 "Why Trump Killed TPP—and Why it Matters to You."

NBC News, January 23, 2017.

Reichmann, Deb. 2020 "Trump disbanded NSC pandemic unit that experts had praised." AP News, March 14, 2020

Roberson, Lori. 2019. "Trump's Mixed Record on Gun Control."
FactCheck-

.Org, August 8, 2019. https://www.factcheck.org/2019/08/
trumps-mixed-[1] record-on-gun-control/

Rogers, James. 2017. "Understanding the Conservative Split Over
Globaliza- tion." Law and Liberty, December 20, 2017.

Rothman, Lily. 2018 "The Story Behind George H.W. Bush's Famous
'Read My Lips, No New Taxes' Promise" Time, December 1, 2018.

Savage, David G. 2019 "DACA timeline: The rise and resilience of the
'Dreamers' program." Los Angeles Times, November 19, 2019

Silva, Derek. 2021. "Who benefited most from the Tax Cuts and Jobs
Act??

Polygenius, December 28, 2021.

Swanson, Anna, and Tankersly, Jim. 2020. "Trump Just Signed the

U.S.M.C.A. Here's What's in the New NAFTA." The New York Times,
January 29, 2020.

Thompson, Frank. 2020. "Six Ways the Trump Administration Sabotaged
the ACA." Brookings, October 9, 2020.

University of California at Santa Barbara, 2023. "The American President
Project." January 28, 2023.

\arroli, Jim. 2018. "President Trump Criticises Federal Reserve For Raising
Interest Rates." NPR, July 19, 2018.

\ahn, Max. 2023. "A timeline of the Silicon Valley Bank collapse." ABC
News, March 14m 2023.

---

1. http://www.factcheck.org/2019/08/trumps-mixed-